EUROPE BEYOND MOBILITY

Mobility, which has represented a critical scientific category and political driver, is currently under strong public scrutiny: has mobility lost its potential for social cohesion and political integration? *Europe Beyond Mobility: Mobilities, Social Cohesion and Political Integration* assesses this question by focusing on the European integration process, conceptualized as a political project for the promotion of different flows of mobility.

Mobility has been a fundamental tool for territorial strength and political integration among European countries. Based on a realistic understanding of the potentials and limits of mobility, this book pleads for a "resonant mobility" in the interest of a renovated European integration process. It examines how, in opposition to those advocating for national borders and mobility restrictions, the EU needs to explore new regulatory models which limit mobility's adverse social, economic and environmental impacts and make accessible the benefits of alternative flow models. It also provides an analytical framework for the study of current trends of mobility limitation, migration restriction and re-bordering, and offers a complementary and innovative framework for the study of globalization.

Europe Beyond Mobility will be of interest to academics and students as well as policy makers and practitioners internationally in the fields of mobility, migration and border studies.

Vincent Kaufmann is Associate Professor of Urban Sociology and Mobility at École Polytechnique Fédérale de Lausanne (EPFL). Since 2011, he is also scientific director of the Mobile Lives Forum in Paris. After a master's degree in sociology (University of Geneva), he did his PhD at EPFL on rationalities underlying transport modal practices. He has been an invited lecturer at Lancaster University (2000–2001), École des Ponts et Chaussées, Paris (2001–2002), Laval University, Québec (2008), Nimegen University (2010), Université de Toulouse Le Mirail (2011), Politechnico Milan (2016), Université Catholique de Louvain (2004–2018) and Tongji University in Shanghai (2018).

Ander Audikana is Master Class Seal of Excellence Research Fellow at the Department of Architecture and Urban Studies (DAStU), Politecnico di Milano (Italy). He obtained a B.A. in sociology at the University of Deusto, a M.A. in city and regional planning at the University Paris 12 and the ENS Diploma in urban sociology at the École Normale Supérieure de Paris. He holds a PhD in sociology from the University Paris-Est. He was Fulbright-Schuman scholar in urban planning in the United States at George Mason University and at the University of California, Berkeley. He was also postdoctoral research fellow at the École Polytechnique Fédérale de Lausanne and the University of Deusto.

Guillaume Drevon is currently working at the Luxembourg Institute of Socio-Economic Research – LISER – since 2021 as a research associate. Guillaume Drevon is also an associate scientist at the Urban Sociology Lab of the Swiss Federal Institute of Technology Lausanne. He obtained a B.A. in geography and a M.A. in territorial development and planning at the University of Grenoble-Alpes. He obtained an AFR-PHD grant from the Luxembourg National Research Fund. He holds a PhD in geography from the University of Grenoble-Alpes in partnership with the Luxembourg Institute of Socio-economic Research. A part of his research focuses on cross-border regions by developing an individual centered approach which reveals socio-spatial bridges across the border (attachment, identities, personal network, cross-border activities, cross-border past experiences).

EUROPE BEYOND MOBILITY

Mobilities, Social Cohesion and Political Integration

Vincent Kaufmann, Ander Audikana and Guillaume Drevon
Translated from French by Jessica Strelec

Routledge
Taylor & Francis Group
NEW YORK AND LONDON

First published 2022
by Routledge
605 Third Avenue, New York, NY 10158

and by Routledge
2 Park Square, Milton Park, Abingdon, Oxon, OX14 4RN

Routledge is an imprint of the Taylor & Francis Group, an informa business

Library of Congress Cataloging-in-Publication Data
Names: Kaufmann, Vincent, author. | Audikana, Ander, 1983- author. | Drevon, Guillaume, author.
Title: Europe beyond mobility : mobilities, social cohesion and political integration / Vincent Kaufmann, Ander Audikana and Guillaume Drevon ; translated from French by Jessica Strelec.
Description: New York, NY : Routledge, 2022. | Series: Networked urban mobilities | Includes bibliographical references and index. |
Identifiers: LCCN 2021025934 (print) | LCCN 2021025935 (ebook) | ISBN 9780367343231 (hbk) | ISBN 9780367343224 (pbk) | ISBN 9780429325014 (ebk)
Subjects: LCSH: European Union countries—Economic conditions. | Europe—Economic integration. | European Union countries—Social conditions. | Freedom of movement—European Union countries. | Social mobility—European Union countries. | Social integration—European Union countries.
Classification: LCC HC241.2 .K295 2022 (print) | LCC HC241.2 (ebook) | DDC 330.94—dc23
LC record available at https://lccn.loc.gov/2021025934
LC ebook record available at https://lccn.loc.gov/2021025935

ISBN: 978-0-367-34323-1 (hbk)
ISBN: 978-0-367-34322-4 (pbk)
ISBN: 978-0-429-32501-4 (ebk)

DOI: 10.4324/9780429325014

Typeset in Bembo
by Apex CoVantage, LLC

The preparation of this book received support from the Swiss National Science Foundation (SNSF): grant number: 179555.

CONTENTS

1

CITY EUROPA

Europe has become one (very) big city, with rich and poor neighborhoods, outskirts and centers, and, above all, urban issues. In reality, Europe may have always been a megacity, but recent changes and their impact have made this analogy clearer and more pertinent than ever.

As with all cities, it is not easy to delineate the boundaries of the European metropolis. Europe indeed remains an ill-defined, vague geographic space whose borders are malleable and fluctuate with the vagaries of geopolitics. Moreover, it seems to be spreading, much as urbanization is advancing towards the outskirts of cities. New spaces join and merge with the urban continent functionally, new neighborhoods appear, and the urban perimeter expands, thus creating urban sprawl. However, Europe is also shrinking, for example with the United Kingdom's exit following the Brexit vote on 23 June 2016.

Like cities ravaged by hurricanes, floods, eruptions, earthquakes, fires and wars, Europe, too, could lose part of its territory, as eurozone and Schengen Area crises suggest. This situation has already left some neighborhoods adrift. *City Europa*, it seems, has a core that mutates according to its peripheral areas to the north, south and east. It is not, however, a large, isolated city in the center of the world and could never become one, as the center of the world, we are told, is now in Asia.

City Europa is a city that by nature is cosmopolitan and extremely varied. Its inhabitants speak different languages and have specific religious affiliations, regional and national traditions, and diverse lifestyles. What is more, most people in this big city are very much attached to their neighborhoods, where they have established strong ties over generations. The neighborhood conflicts and violence that have erupted throughout its history have sent shockwaves across the planet.

In recent decades, the number of meeting places in *City Europa* has steadily climbed (universities, markets, beaches, train stations, airports, etc.). Concurrently, exchanges between inhabitants have intensified without necessarily becoming

DOI: 10.4324/9780429325014-1

generalized. The latter have come to know and even, in some cases, love one another through such exchange. Yet, tensions persist between the different neighborhoods and are growing. Thus, while it is the variety and intensity of exchanges that give big cities their character, these exchanges are also the catalyst for the most passionate neighborhood conflicts.

Managing *City Europa*'s neighborhood conflicts is not the job of any single government; many different actors are involved in governing this great city. Certain institutions of metropolitan rank have appropriated the name "Europe." While some are becoming increasingly powerful, none has complete control over *City Europa's* problems because none can lay claim to the entire metropolitan territory. Some neighborhoods effectively prefer not to incorporate metropolitan institutions or seek to limit their participation to certain sectors. As such, each district still has considerable autonomy when it comes to acting on behalf of its own territory. At the same time, however, action at the metropolitan level can still influence the "local" politics of each neighborhood.

When we look closely at *City Europa*, it also seems obvious that the more central districts have greater influence over the city's future, while smaller or outlying ones have a harder time making their voices heard.

Cities are characterized not only by their territory, their social and economic diversity, and their specific scales of government, but also by the fact that their inhabitants face common problems, which leads us to consider Europe as one giant metropolis. This does not mean the problems are the same for everyone, nor that they manifest themselves everywhere in the same way. Some neighborhoods are better equipped than others or are in a better position to cope with potential problems. However, when confronted with famine, flu, plague, fires or violence, no European inhabitant feels (or would feel) entirely safe.

In *Europa*, what ultimately connects different neighborhoods, unites the most diverse entities and pools local governability strategies is a long list of common problems. This book aims specifically to explore *City Europa* and to address it from the particular angle of mobility – the catalyst of many of its issues. It is the fruit of the work of three European researchers, Spanish, French and Swiss respectively, who met at the EPFL Urban Sociology Laboratory in Lausanne, Switzerland. Specialists in the fields of human geography, political sociology and urban sociology, all three are also active in the field of urban studies and of mobility more specifically. Their respective work shows that, over the past 15 years, mobility has become an increasingly relevant phenomenon in urban dynamics and has brought about profound change since the 1970s. Driven by the potential speed of transport and communication systems, mobility has spread, globalized and fragmented. Beyond the mosaic of terminology and wealth of approaches, this shift does not blur differences; on the contrary, it accentuates and fortifies them based on new criteria such as mobility.

The movement of people, goods, capital and ideas is clearly at the heart of global changes in *City Europa* and affects all aspects of economic, political and social life. The shrinking of time and space and the relaxing of regulations with regard to the movement of people, goods and capital have had a major impact on societies and their territories, with the mobility of factors of production increasing considerably. In terms of capital, mobility has been concurrent with the development of the financial industry and booming returns. Liberalization, the development of information and communication technology and the ongoing development of new services by the financial industry have given rise to extremely rapid capital flows on a global scale. In daily life, the opportunities afforded by rapid transit systems were acclaimed by the population, which uses them not only intensively but often in ways that differ from those originally conceptualized by their designers. Cities are now traversed by considerable speed differentials, which are ultimately an essential vector of their cosmopolitanism.

In a very concrete way, the book you are holding in your hands follows on from several research projects carried out conjointly by the three authors: theoretical work on the concepts of mobility and motility (Drevon, Gerber, & Kaufmann, 2020; Kaufmann, 2011; Kaufmann & Audikana, 2020), research on cross-border commons in Europe funded by the Swiss National Science Foundation and a survey of political controversies around mobility in Switzerland, which was the subject of a book published in 2017 (Kaufmann & Audikana, 2017).

In fact, social crises directly linked to mobility are coming thicker and faster: the pressing demand for the right to amble in Taksim Square in 2013, the cry for public transport versus Olympic Game funding in Rio in 2016, the rejection of speed limitations and carbon taxes by the Yellow Vests in winter 2018, the general strike in Chile following the increase subway tickets prices in October 2019 and, in 2020, the forced immobilization of a good part of the planet to fight against the spread of COVID-19.

All are signs that highlight mobility's role as an organizing agent of society and the urgent need to rethink it. Curiously, little research thus far has addressed these issues from a mobility perspective. Implicitly taking for granted article 13 of the Universal Declaration of Human Rights, which states that every person has the right to move freely, many works are based on the more or less explicit assumption that increases in flows are a "mere" reflection of the democratization of the right to "free" movement, which is considered a natural right.

Some of *City Europa*'s problems are directly related to mobility. Immigrants who arrive in Lampedusa and Idomeni are part of a south-north migratory flow that structures the relationship between *City Europa* and one of its "suburbs" on the southern shore of the Mediterranean. The circulation of currency – which can also be seen as a form of mobility – in search of havens safe from market developments is another problem. On another note, the flight from Amsterdam to Kuala Lumpur full of passengers traveling on business and for pleasure that was shot down over the Ukraine is also a paradigmatic example of the systemic importance of mobility in our societies.

Ultimately, *City Europa*'s evolution and development are inseparable from contemporary mobilities. In this book, we would like to go even further and suggest that its construction is based on a conscious political strategy to increase flows between different neighborhoods, banking on the fact that increasing exchanges will allow for greater inclusion of the parties. This process would ultimately strengthen cohesion and allow for the forging of a true common identity. If we adhere to this hypothesis, Europe would actually create mobility.

This hypothesis seems particularly relevant for that institutional scale that is primarily responsible for governing *City Europa*: the European Union (EU). The EU has become so central to city governance that, in their usage, the terms "Europe" and "EU" have become synonymous. While admitting that "Europe" refers to a broader, more complex reality than the "EU," our remarks will essentially be structured relative to the latter. We will focus notably on the strategic goal of promoting increased mobility within *City Europa* as led by EU.

In addition to this hypothesis, our research on urban mobility demonstrates that mobility is fundamentally ambivalent: it can undoubtedly be a vector for reinforcing cohesion but can also be at the root of renewed tension and conflict. The building of an airport or of a road through a neighborhood, traffic, security, noise and pollution, the loss of a certain local "soul" due to more traffic, the increase in highly mobile individuals (people who work several hundred kilometers from their primary residence) are all potential sources of fragmentation and weakened cohesion and are all linked to mobility. Faced with these threats, inhabitants of big cities usually try to protect themselves as much as possible. This is reflected in the often strong opposition to the construction of new infrastructure, the installation of anti-noise panels, the prohibition of transit in many neighborhoods and the increase in gated communities with private security patrols. This desire to "protect ourselves" incites us to avoid certain routes or places at certain times of the day. In all of these cases, mobility is not experienced as a vector of inclusion but rather as a dynamic that puts inhabitants of big cities at risk, an out-of-control force that raises numerous issues.

With these observations, we concur with sociologist George Simmel (1950, p. 416) when he suggested that life in the big cities gives rise to a "reserved character" marked not only by indifference but also by "a faint aversion, reciprocal strangeness and repudiation" due to an increase in encounters. However, he goes on to say that, directly or indirectly, all strategies to avoid contact have an integrative function:

> A latent antipathy and the preparatory stage of practical antagonism effect the distances and aversions without which this mode of life could not at all be led. The extent and the mixture of this style of life, the rhythm of its emergence and disappearance, the forms in which it is satisfied – all these, with the unifying motives in the narrower sense, form the inseparable whole of the metropolitan style of life. What appears in the metropolitan style of life directly as dissociation is in reality only one of its elemental forms of socialization.
>
> *(Simmel, 1950, p. 416)*

In recent years, avoidance tactics have been on the rise in *City Europa*. A certain "reserve" or "indifference" towards the inhabitants of other neighborhoods and towards EU metropolitan institutions is gaining ground and is accompanied by pessimistic rhetoric and fear. Some suggest reforming EU metropolitan institutions while others seemingly want to eradicate them, considering them to be the cause of the problem. Some argue for a "return to neighborhoods," others point out that neighborhoods have become too small to face the challenges that plague big cities. Thus are the integral promises linked to greater mobility called into question.

Starting from the metaphor of Europe as a continent-city, this book addresses the social and political integration process by applying theoretical and analytical tools derived from urban and mobility studies. The integration of the "European metropolis" has been historically promoted by European institutions through policies that seek to intensify mobility flows. The process of European integration has been conceived in this perspective to promote different types of mobility without systematically considering the impact. Based on these considerations, the book aims to rethink mobility policies in Europe in order to shape another Europe.

It begins with a theoretical chapter that aims to define the notion of mobility in a broad way, and in so doing provides a framework for analyzing political ideologies relative to different types of mobility (reversible, irreversible, materiel, immaterial), and ranging from ultra-liberal to isolationist positions.

Based on the theoretical considerations raised, Chapter 3 analyzes the links between the European integration process and the promotion of different mobility flows. Over its history, the EU has conceived and implemented different policy interventions oriented towards promoting transnational mobility. Three types of interventions are distinguished: 1) regulatory policies, which have attempted to create a common framework as regards the technical and juridical conditions of mobility; 2) investment policies, which have aimed to equip the European territory with new infrastructures and spatial interventions; and 3) incentive policies, which provide the resources for developing mobility skills and support the mobility strategies of individual and collective actors.

Chapter 4 explores the effects of the mobility policies in Europe described in Chapter 3 on individuals' lifestyles and travel patterns. Based on the results of several major surveys, it shows how mobility has gradually been transformed from a freedom to travel fast and far to an obligation for those who simply wish to work. This reversal is dramatic, and people who move fast, far and frequently generally feel their lifestyle is a constraint from which they cannot escape. Freedom of movement has thus become an obligation to move.

The book continues by exploring mobility in European cross-border areas. Cross-border areas have traditionally been considered as advanced laboratories of the European integration process where debordering practices and cosmopolitan identities are believed to emerge. However, they are also spaces where re-bordering dynamics exist and national identities are reaffirmed.

Chapter 6 explores the reasons and arguments commonly given for opposing mobility policies and practices. These range from ethical considerations to environmental arguments and include economic, ethnic and planning concerns. The chapter provides a comprehensive overview of anti-mobility political discourses in Europe based on several sectors, namely large transport infrastructures, anti-immigration, anti-tourism movements and health crises. The analysis investigates the common points and divergences of anti-mobility movement proponents.

This analysis continues in Chapter 7 with the case study of Switzerland. The Swiss context is characterized by a high level of international openness with regard to the mobility of objects, capital and services, which contrasts policies aimed at limiting the mobility and urbanization process internally. In addition, the country is prone to strong immigration and cross-border flows. As such, the Swiss context favors the emergence of innovative political initiatives and policy solutions in the area of mobility.

Finally, a concluding chapter questions the extent to which the European integration project can be dissociated from the idea of increasing mobility. Should this project be based on alternative approaches? Should the mobility approach be supplemented by other factors such as slowness, proximity and local rooting?

References

Drevon, G., Gerber, P., & Kaufmann, V. (2020). Dealing with daily rhythms: Families' strategies to tackle chronic time pressure. *Sustainability*, *12*, 7193.

Kaufmann, V. (2011). *Rethinking the city: Urban dynamics and motility*. Lausanne: Routledge; EPFL Press.

Kaufmann, V., & Audikana, A. (2017). *Mobilité et libre circulation en Europe: Un regard suisse*. Paris: Economica.

Kaufmann, V., & Audikana, A. (2020). Mobility capital and motility. In O. B. Jensen, C. Lassen, V. Kaufmann, M. Freudendal-Pedersen, & I. S. Gøtzsche Lange (Eds.), *Handbook of urban mobilities* (1st ed., pp. 41–47). New York: Routledge.

Simmel, G. (1950). *The sociology of Georg Simmel*. New York: The Free Press.

2

MOBILITY, SOCIAL COHESION AND POLITICS

Introduction

This theoretical chapter retraces the relationship between mobility, social cohesion and politics by drawing on sociological and geographical approaches. Mobility has traditionally been conceptualized as a driver or accelerator of social integration processes and geographical integration. However, the environmental, spatial and social issues that stem from increasing levels of mobility have largely been underestimated. This chapter provides a more balanced overview of the benefits and challenges relative to mobility. It also provides a framework for analyzing the political ideologies linked to different types of mobility (reversible, irreversible, materiel, immaterial), and ranging from ultra-liberal to isolationist.

In the context of globalization and economic regionalization, the process of European integration has led to a loss of border control and the riddance of barriers to the free movement of goods, services and people. The European Union (EU) itself can be seen as a "human mobility system" (Recchi, 2015, p. 145) resulting from the encouragement of different types of cross-border mobility. The right to free movement is a fundamental aspect of European citizenship, even if it remains limited in practice for specific social categories (Favell, 2008; Fligstein, 2008). Cross-border mobility plays two key roles with respect to the EU: on one hand, European institutions have conceived transnational mobility as a tool to strengthen territorial and political integration between different European countries; on the other hand, individual mobility has been presented as a way to develop professional capacities and training, and in so doing achieve social cohesion.

The promotion of cross-border mobility can be understood as a debordering strategy towards a borderless Europe (Recchi, 2019), which "can itself be seen as a borderland" (Delanty & Rumford, 2005, p. 188). The notions of bordering, debordering and rebordering have been extensively used over the last two decades

DOI: 10.4324/9780429325014-2

to highlight the processual and historically contingent dimension of borders and to overcome state-centric approaches (Newman, 2006; Rumford, 2006; Van Houtum & Van Naerssen, 2002). In this respect, European integration can be conceptualized as a functional (e.g., the elimination of economic and commercial barriers) and constructionist (e.g., the creation of shared experiences through exchange programs) debordering process designed to create a common European identity. Bordering dynamics relative to the European integration process operate at different levels: some are virtual and deterritorialized (via media, social networks, bordering technologies, etc.), and are diffused throughout the society (Balibar, 2003). In parallel, some specific sites such as large European cosmopolitan cities and border areas, which are characterized by relatively high levels of cross-border mobility and exchange, are particularly affected by bordering dynamics. It is generally assumed that the daily cross-border experience of European integration (Kuhn, 2011) can favor cosmopolitan attitudes and shared identifications. However, it is equally possible and historically observable that cities and cross-border areas are hotspots for the emergence and spread of nationalistic attitudes. Higher levels of cross-border mobility and exchange in border areas can, for instance, have ambivalent effects that can entail both opportunities and vulnerabilities for their inhabitants (Durand, Decoville, & Knippschild, 2020). Under the institutionalized Europhoria, a Europhobia may be latent (Dürrschmidt, 2006).

Sociological approaches in European studies (Fligstein, 2008; Kuhn, 2015; Mau, 2012; Recchi, 2015; Recchi et al., 2019) have investigated the link between individual cross-border mobility debordering practices (transnationalism) and the emergence of cosmopolitan or European identification. Higher levels of transnational practices are thought to enhance identification with supranational scales of belonging. As stated by Fligstein (2008, p. 16): "a European identity is first and foremost going to arise among people who associate with each other across national boundaries." Highly mobile transnational elites seem to develop a deeper identification with Europe compared to nationally oriented individuals whose transnational experience is comparatively more limited (Favell, 2008; Fligstein, 2008). Nevertheless, supranational European identifications do not necessarily lead to the abandoning of local ties, and even the "Eurostar" elites (Favell, 2008) living in large, globalized cities appear to be deeply rooted at the local level (Andreotti, Le Galès, & Moreno Fuentes, 2015). Instead, European citizens seem to have developed different levels of belonging that correspond to the European system of multilevel governance.

Defining and Describing Mobilities

In this respect, mobility is a cornerstone of the European integration process and has clear political significance. But what is mobility? The concept of mobility is defined in multiple ways depending on the discipline. In a very general way, the term describes a process of change that distinguishes the behaviors or trajectories of individual and/or collective actors, goods, information or capital (Gallez & Kaufmann, 2009). When used to describe a person, group of people or company, mobility refers to movement in geographical space. In this case, mobility applies to changes of residence (migratory movement, residential moves, etc.) as well as travel for activities outside the home (business trips, home-work commutes, etc.), depending on the timeframe of the analysis. However, the concept of mobility can also refer to a self-transformation (a change of role, professional status or social position) that involves no geographical movement whatsoever. In this second perspective, social mobility refers to a change of position (of individuals or social groups) in social space. When referring to merchandise, mobility concerns both tangible and intangible goods (freight and capital mobility respectively). Fourth and finally, mobility refers to remote communication. Hence, the term "virtual mobility" is used to refer to live remote interaction between people.

This wealth of precise, sector-specific definitions is not an asset when it comes to addressing mobility: on the contrary, it hinders mobility's ability to exist as a clearly articulated political issue. And yet, mobility is a powerful indicator of the web of paradoxes in which contemporary globalized societies are trapped, the first of which is the imagery of freedom inherent to the notion of mobility in the Western imagery.

Since the early 2000s, a great deal of thinking on the question of mobility has been done under the banner of the "mobility turn" (Sheller & Urry, 2006), the goal being to establish an all-inclusive definition of the phenomenon so as to forge a real concept. This thinking is mainly geared toward a theoretical understanding of the phenomenon (Cresswell, 2006; Urry, 2007), of how mobilities are experienced (Merriman, 2012), of the role they play in individuals' development today (Kellerman, 2006), of how they have evolved over time, etc. These works stress the fact that movement in physical space is often a means for achieving a specific goal and not usually a goal in itself, and that it is therefore essential to consider the nature of this goal in order to understand the drivers and motivations behind mobility.

Michel Bassand and Marie-Claude Brulhardt (1980), Bertrand Montulet (1998), Luc Boltanski and Eve Chiapello (1999) and Zygmunt Bauman (2000) ascribe important developments to the notion of mobility which, for them, is a discussion that goes far beyond physical movement in geographic space. Following these authors, we consider mobility as "an intention to and the subsequent act of moving in geographical space that in one way or another is associated with the self-transformation of the actors or objects concerned." This definition allows us to approach mobility as a socio-spatial phenomenon, an analytical indicator and, finally, as a social norm and value. These three facets of the mobility concept are both specific and complementary. We will now consider them individually in greater detail, starting with the mobility of people, which can also describe the mobility of tangible and intangible objects and capital.

Mobility as a Social Phenomenon

The first observation is that "being mobile" actually refers to two things. The first is moving or changing location. It also refers to self-transformation, adapting to new situations, changing status, positions, skills, etc. These two dimensions are strongly intertwined (Mincke & Kaufmann, 2017). In contemporary societies, which are characterized by the globalization of trade, mobility is often presented as an important condition for social integration, especially as regards access to jobs and careers. Thus, for instance, upward professional mobility within a company (characterized most notably by an increase in revenue) tends to influence the choice of holiday destinations and leisure mobility in general. Another example is changing jobs and, thus, workplace locations and consequently mobility patterns (longer/shorter daily commute distance, job-related travel, mode of transport used).

Things have changed considerably since Pitirim Sorokin's early works on American society in the 1920s, particularly with regard to the analysis of intergenerational socio-professional mobility grid tables and their structure (see Cuin, 1993; Wright, Costello, Hachen, & Sprague, 1982). In this work, changes in socio-professional status based on social origin was considered a key indicator of a society's meritocratic nature. Industrial society has, from its inception, valued social mobility because the dynamics of collective change are based on individuals' desire to improve their socio-economic condition. In this perspective, everyone invests in production in the hopes of improving their living conditions and social status on the basis of merit. This idea is based on two principles: the first affirms individual freedom in defining and enacting the quest for status; the second calls for equality among individuals so that one's status of origin is no longer an obstacle to the desired upward social mobility. Paradoxically, it is first and foremost a question of maintaining egalitarian rhetoric in a competition for statuses which, by definition, are unequal. The paradox is generally erased by the implementation of measures to ensure baseline equality for the different actors according to their social origin.

While these considerations do not explicitly include space, authors started highlighting the fact that spatial mobility was becoming increasingly important – even central – to socio-professional careers as early as the 1980s. Thus, Manuel Castells (1996) and later Zygmunt Bauman (2000) noted that individuals are more or less attached to the local world in which they live depending on their professional status, and that this attachment is a key factor in their potential for social mobility. Michel Bassand and Marie-Claude Brulhardt (1980) show that ascending professional paths requires specific spatial mobility depending on the area of origin (central or peripheral). Gil Viry and his colleagues (Viry & Kaufmann, 2015) went one step further by highlighting the existence of an injunction to spatial mobility in view of labor market competition. Nowadays, the issue is less about highlighting social inequalities than about social mobility potential or condemning fast-paced lifestyles due to this "mobility injunction" (Drevon, Gwiazdzinski, & Kaufmann, 2019; Mincke & Montulet, 2019).

Mobility as an Analytical Indicator

The second observation is that mobility can be considered an analytical indicator of social reality. In this sense, measuring mobility can, for example, help us understand family dynamics. It can also highlight the chronic time pressures on women with young children and daily challenges in terms of reconciling family, social and professional life.

Approaching mobility as an analytical indicator involves three dimensions (for more, see Kaufmann, 2011):

- The range of possibilities. Every situation has a given range of possibilities in terms of mobility based on a specific set of contextual elements, including available networks (road, highway, rail networks, airport platforms, telecommunications, etc.); the development, performance and conditions of access; geographical space and territorial configurations (urban configurations, density of amenities, institutional divisions, etc.); the labor market (training/employment opportunities, unemployment rate); the institutions and laws that govern human activities (family policy, property and housing subsidies and immigration policy) – in short, all of the economic/social relationships and success models a society upholds and the way actors are tested in order to succeed.
- Motility, i.e., the ability to move. Each actor, object (tangible or otherwise) and piece of information is characterized by its own motility. This motility concerns geographic, economic and social space.
- Travel, i.e., getting around in space, or more specifically the way of arranging what is close, what is connected and what moves.

These three dimensions together produce mobility. However, it is important not to make assumptions about their relationships with one another. A broad range of possibilities does not necessarily result in a given degree of appropriation or uses. Similarly, highly developed motility within a population may anchor individuals to their territory rather than help them focus on self-transformation. Motility can also remain in a latent state and not be activated. A population that travels a great deal does not necessarily have a highly developed range of possibilities for travel.

An empirical analysis of mobility as an analytical indicator highlights an essential point: that the modern world is marked by increasing reversible mobilities (Viry & Kaufmann, 2015). Reversible mobilities are roundtrips made within a short timeframe. Such mobilities are contrasted with irreversible mobilities, which are trips that do not involve an immediate return and, in some cases, no return at all. Reversibility and irreversibility must therefore be seen as ideal-types – two extremes of a continuum in which mobility practices can be understood – as purely reversible or irreversible forms of mobility do not exist.

Among the most irreversible forms of mobility are certain types of international migration. International migration almost inevitably involves change – cultural, linguistic, institutional, etc. Forced residential mobility, like a prison sentence, is in another register, irreversible mobility for the detainee (Mincke & Montulet, 2019). A prison sentence marks an individual's identity definitively if for no other reason than that a criminal record follows a person their whole life. Irreversible forms of mobility are not necessarily experienced as a constraint, however. Thus, while irreversibility implies a marked change of context and of the person's identity, these changes can also be opted for and appreciated as an exploration or new direction.

Reversible mobility, on the other hand, is a social experience that can be more easily aborted and changes the individual's life relatively little. The most reversible mobilities are repetitive and routine and fall within the category of "non-events." Daily commuting and business travel are good examples of forms of daily professional mobility. Thus, one should not assume that because a person commutes to work each day but does not remember the details of each trip, or because an international consultant often makes long-distance business trips but does not remember the specifics, that these forms of reversible mobility have no impact on their identity; on the contrary, their repetitive nature often structures an individual's identity, both for the individual him or herself and for outside observers (family, friends, colleagues, etc.). On the other hand, when such experiences cease, one can imagine they did little to change the lives of those in question, or at least less so in any case than irreversible mobility.

Research shows that the concepts of reversibility and irreversibility help in highlighting several important phenomena as applies to mobility (Ravalet, Vincent-Geslin, Kaufmann, Viry, & Dubois, 2015):

- Reversible mobility seems to be highly valued in contemporary transport and mobility policies. For example, European policy has until now focused on promoting reversible mobility through the construction of major infrastructure such as a pan-European TGV and highway network, as well as investments in airport platforms. In the dominant imaginary, mobility = promotion of reversibility.
- Reversibility does not necessarily reflect the aspirations of the entire population, as a growing desire to slow down and live locally indicates. The ability to disconnect or uproot and re-root elsewhere is valued by certain people and groups to the point of forming specific mobility habits and thereby reflecting irreversibility.
- Reversibility helps in understanding inequalities relative to mobility. Reversibility raises questions of inequality insofar as it entails having access to a number of technical systems (rapid transport, remote communication, etc.) and having certain skills. The actors' potential for reversibility is, in fact, an excellent indicator of inequalities in the face of mobility.

Mobility as a Social Norm

The description above presents mobility as a staple (Gallez, 2015) per its definition in Article 13 of the Universal Declaration of Human Rights relative to freedom of movement. Mobility has also become a dominant social norm in contemporary Western societies (Mincke & Montulet, 2019), notably based on an imaginary that associates rapid, long-distance journeys (and reversible mobilities more generally) with the process of the democratization of mobility. With the possibility of travelling great distances at great speeds, individuals are free to establish the desired contacts with no barriers in space or time. Such rhetoric suggests that those most likely to occupy the most desirable social statuses are those most willing to comply with a logic of unfettered flexibility. Thus, the particularity of this ideology consists in accepting that, through a shift in meaning, mobility in physical space naturally favors the fair distribution of individuals within societies. It would therefore suffice to promote spatial accessibility in order to create social equality. By this interpretation, the major developments in reversible, rapid, long-distance mobilities that global societies are currently experiencing is a clear indication of a shift towards a more just world.

The rise in reversible mobility illustrates the fact that in contemporary societies, certain forms of mobility have gradually become a standard, an injunction to which individuals must submit. Fast, frequent, long-distance trips are thus a valued form of travel.

While this injunction concerns all spheres of activity (Mincke & Montulet, 2019), it is particularly marked in the work world. Nowadays, one must be able to travel fast, often and far in order to land and keep a job or to change jobs, but also to prove that you have had international work experience, or more simply a good vacation (Le Breton, 2005). In other words, in today's world, adhering to social norms has become an injunction to practice reversible mobility.

In the work world, this injunction has resulted in an increase in travel (home to work commutes, job-related travel, visiting clients or colleagues, etc.) and jobs with no fixed workplace and that are structurally mobile (Gay, Kaufmann, & Landriève, 2021):

- Home to work commutes are increasingly long due to the increase in transport speeds and more and more frequent due to flexible working hours in certain professions or residential choices that lead to long-distance commuting (3–4 hours of transport a day).
- Business travel is becoming more frequent. Nowadays, such travel is not reserved for top executives and salespeople, but middle managers of large companies as well.
- The number of mobile workstations is increasing with the explosion of the road transport and logistics sector (drivers, delivery people). More generally, the ranks of "mobile workers" (once seasonal or fairgrounds employees) have been joined by posted workers and travelers.

Concretely, reversible mobility seems to be the adjustment variable when it comes to freedom of residential choice and freedom to create businesses. For example, the "high mobility" of those who move fast, far and often for work is becoming the norm: one in two working people in Europe must accept this lifestyle at some point in their career (Ravalet et al., 2015). It should also be noted that the same research also shows that high mobility practices can be useful when it comes to finding or keeping a job: 80% of highly-mobile Spanish workers surveyed in a European research study considered that they had kept or gotten a job thanks to some form of high mobility (2012 survey following the 2008 crisis – Ravalet et al., 2015).

The Promotion of Reversible Mobility and Its Consequences

The different facets of the notion of mobility we have just presented illustrate its plasticity. Mobility emerges as one of the core values of our contemporary societies. A classic and celebrated example of this is the figure of the creative neo-nomad who works in the digital or design industry, traveling from airport to airport across the world. All of this clearly indicates a reversal: mobility – a value associated with freedom of movement – has gradually and in different ways become a requisite and a social norm associated with reversibility to be complied with.

Tim Cresswell (2006) has worked extensively on the question of mobility as a norm that produces injunctions. For him, mobility is a social product that must be thought of as an intertwining of physical movement, meaning and practice in a context of power. In his work, he shows that the images, narratives and values associated with travel and movement vary in a given society in space or in time. For example, in the 19th century, the mobility of workers was seen as dangerous and a potential source of public disorder. As such, attempts were made to control it. Today, conversely, the movement of workers within the EU is highly valued. The value given to movement also varies within a same given society. For example, while the mobility of web nomads is highly valued, that of immigrants raises fears that are expressed through metaphors such as "flooding" or "submersion."

Our systems of travel as such do not create freely moving flows that circulate without resistance, as Manuel Castells (1996) suggested. On the contrary, there is constant friction and turbulence in the world of mobility. According to him, this turbulence is not the product of the failure of mobility systems; it is an intrinsic and unpredictable aspect of it that affects the pace at which we move and path we take. At the same time, this turbulence affects people's daily lives by putting them under constant pressure and in a state of chronic stress. But here again, differences in income level play a key role in cushioning (or not) the effects of this turbulence. Being able to take a taxi when there is a public transport breakdown, hire a babysitter to pick up the children from school, etc. can make a major difference in the quality of individuals' lives.

Motility and the Politics of Mobility

Insofar as mobility is critical for social integration, and as the ability to move is not necessarily equally distributed, the political and ideological nature of mobility becomes clearer. The concept of motility allows us to investigate the inequalities associated with mobility patterns and to examine their political and ideological connotations. Motility can be defined as a specific set of characteristics that allows actors to be mobile (or not) to varying degrees. Motility includes 1) social conditions of access (i.e. the conditions under which actors can utilize the transport offer in the broadest sense), 2) the knowledge and skills required to use the transport offer, and 3) mobility aspirations (i.e. actual use of the transport offer that enables users to realize these aspirations). Motility is location specific; every territory has a specific range of possibilities and potential when it comes to creating opportunities to move. What determines this range of possibilities and receptiveness to projects largely has to do with the material and immaterial conditions of each specific context. Any action is therefore location specific as well and requires an environment that provides footholds. The concept of motility has been extensively discussed in the literature over the last two decades (Kesselring, 2006; Söderström & Crot, 2010; Jensen, 2006; Nowicka, 2006; Sheller, 2011; Merriman, 2012).

Expanding our motility is thus an inherent part of a major societal transformation, and the capacity to be mobile – i.e. motility – is becoming a sort of "capital" in its own right. This "capital" is more than a mere combination of income (economic capital), education level (cultural capital) and social networks (social capital). Until the 1970s, professional careers were built on the traditional economic, cultural and social capital we know well. Nowadays, having a career also means being able to play with and have a good command of space in the form of motility. More specifically, it seems that motility helps people to activate other types of capital and thus acts as a "dynamic relay." In many fields, having had at least one professional experience abroad has become indispensable. For those with professional aspirations, success and motility are intrinsically linked, as are the choice to make and realization of such trips.

By distinguishing between different forms of capital (economic, cultural and social), Bourdieu (1986) demonstrated the many mechanisms that regulate the unequal distribution of resources and social reproduction. While acknowledging the key role of economic capital with regard to the dynamics of social structuring, considering complementary forms of capital makes it possible to cope with "economism." While all capital can ultimately be transformed into economic capital through a process of conversion, Bourdieu's analysis offers a finer, richer understanding of how different "capitals" accumulate and merge.

The fundamental issue, therefore, is understanding under what conditions and by what means mobility contributes to the capitalization process in general and promotes dynamics of social integration or exclusion in the long term. Bourdieu (2018) himself introduced the question of mobility as a distinguishing factor in the accumulation process when he asserted that the use of goods and services available in a given space depends both on the capital of the agents and on "the physical distance to these goods" (ibid., p. 109). He also referred to the temporal dimension of mobility in concluding that, because of physical distances, "the power that capital, in its different forms, gives to space is also . . . a power over time" (ibid., p. 111). However, these analyses, which attempt to clarify the link between the "structures of social space" and "structures of physical space", consider space neither as an object of analysis in itself nor as an independent variable strictly speaking. The distribution of capital determines spatial configurations. Economism – the idea that the world can be reduced to money – gives way to sociologism, the idea that the world can be reduced to social relations.

Mobility is therefore at the heart of the struggle for the appropriation of space, if space is truly understood as an issue and not simply a framework. Although much attention has been given to analysing practices and representations of mobility, mobility studies do not seem to have systematically investigated the political significance of mobility. Sheller and Urry (2006, p. 211) suggested that "it is not a question of favoring 'mobile subjectivity,' but rather of monitoring the power of discourses and practices of mobility in creating both movement and stasis." Some scholars admit that "the role of power in mobility" is "still (a) very open question" (Jensen, 2011, p. 255). Söderström et al. (2013, p. 10) considered that, in order to explore the "critical potential of mobility studies," it is necessary to "address explicitly the interplay of mobility and power." Bærenholdt (2013, pp. 20–21) affirmed that there is a "dominating interest in, if not even fascination with, the micro-sociology and phenomenology of mobile practices rather than macro issues" and concludes that "when dealing with issues of power, hegemony and social order, mobility studies are rather vague."

It is undoubtedly Cresswell (2010) who has conceptualized this interplay between mobility and power most aptly in his paper on the politics of mobility. Considering mobility as an entanglement of movement, representation and practice, he explores how and to what extent mobility can be "powerfully political." The author goes beyond the research on mobility inequalities and addresses the question of "how mobility becomes political." While the analytical framework Cresswell proposes is useful in better understanding how mobility becomes a political issue, it does not offer insight on the effects of this evolution in terms of political mobilization.

The literature on technical networks and infrastructures is more relevant to understanding the political effects of mobility issues as it analyses how power is exercised through mobility infrastructures, and how these are eventually contested. Graham and Marvin (2001, p. 392) show that although the "technological mobilities" may contribute to the "secession" or "partition" of metropolitan space, "strategies for resisting" urban splintering can also be constructed. They follow Swyngedouw (1993, p. 195), who suggests that "the changed mobility" "associated with the installation of new mobility commodities and infrastructure may negatively affect the control over place of some while extending the control and power of others." He considers that the accumulation of capital correlates with its circulation, and that, far from being a dependent variable, the control of space plays a key role in this dynamic:

> For each individual, increased mobility is essential to maintain positions of social, economic, political and/or cultural power, while, vice versa, we are

> approaching a condition in which adding to the mobility capacity of one individual may reduce the mobility of all the others.
>
> *(ibid., p. 320)*

Swyngedouw shows that economic and social structuring processes develop "in" and "through" the reconfiguring of space and the transport, communication and mobility patterns associated with them. Considering mobility as both a commodity and a skill, Swyngedouw (ibid., p. 323) concludes that mobility is one of the arenas in which the struggle for power plays out: "social power cannot any longer (if it ever could) be disconnected from the power or ability to move quickly over space." Oosterlynck and Swyngedouw (2010) show how a controversy around air traffic management at Brussels Airport was met with strong local opposition, which annulled the consensual management strategy led by the administration. In this example, a controversy surrounding air traffic management became an opportunity for "proper political engagement" that sought to rebalance inequalities relative to the production and consumption of mobility. Similarly, when Jensen and Richardson (2004, p. 238) introduce the term of "monotopia" – which is defined as a one-dimensional discourse of space through which the construction of seamless networks is promoted – they also consider the "possibilities for new resistance counter-understandings of place." Jensen (2011, p. 268) notes that "as power is always joined by resistance," subjects participate in shaping and making mobility and mobile practices "from below." When investigating the construction of transnational mobile subjects, Jensen and Richardson (2007, p. 148) suggest that such a strategy "should not be read as a full account of the politics of mobility" "but one part of the story of the contested production of future transnational mobility" in which "local struggles and resistances play a part." In this view, the dynamics of domination and resistance seem completely associated, inseparable even.

Therefore, considering mobility as capital not only responds to a need for empirical precision (with regard to the dynamics of accumulation); it also highlights this dimension's increasingly dominant, even discriminating, role in fuelling other capitals (being mobile to earn money, cultivating oneself, or maintaining/expanding social networks). The fundamental contribution of mobility studies consists in giving priority attention to mobility due to its structuring, supra-sectoral nature: "There seems [to be] little doubt that mobility is one of the major resources of 21st-century life and that it is the differential distribution of this resource that produces some of the starkest differences today" (Cresswell, 2010, p. 22).

Ideologies of Mobility

The politics of mobility shed light on an ensemble of ideological tensions that permeate Western societies based on a fundamental dichotomy: considering the mobility of people, goods and capital as a priority response to societal issues or, on the contrary, as a source of problems. In the first case, mobility is synonymous with freedom and is seen as a creative force, whereas in the second case it is perceived as a threat and a destabilizing force. In modern times, mobility has generally been considered synonymous with freedom. More precisely, from a spatial point of view, modern governmentality (Foucault, 2007) seeks to plan a "milieu," which is defined as "that in which circulation is carried out" (ibid., p. 21). Foucault considers circulation as "movement" and a "change of place," as well as "freedom" (ibid., pp. 48–49). Modern apparatuses of governmentality should not control the territory, but rather should maximize the possibilities of mobility/freedom:

> Freedom is nothing else but the correlative of the deployment of apparatuses of security. An apparatus of security . . . cannot operate well except on condition that it is given freedom, in the modern sense [the word] acquires in the eighteenth century: no longer the exemptions and privileges attached to a person, but the possibility of movement, change of place, and processes of circulation of both people and things. I think it is this freedom of circulation, in the broad sense of the term, it is in terms of this option of circulation, that we should understand the word freedom, and understand it as one of the facets, aspects, or dimensions of the deployment of apparatuses of security.
>
> *(ibid., pp. 48–49)*

This fundamental contradiction between two conceptualizations of mobility reflects the dichotomy between reversible and irreversible mobility. Should we promote the cosmopolitism of exchanges through rapid, frequent, long-distance mobility, or should we promote exchanges through irreversible mobility, which implies strong roots in the host society?

It appears that when applied to the movement of people, goods or capital, ideal types of reversible and irreversible mobility often give rise to hybrid positions. One naturally observes two opposing positions at each extreme. On one hand are those favorable to the reversible mobility of people, goods and capital, a position that we will call "ultra-liberal," on the other are those who argue for widespread local rooting and oppose any form of mobility, who we will call "isolationists." However, these positions are theoretical more so than ideological, as identifying positions that are categorically favorable or unfavorable to reversible mobility is difficult.

Between these two extremes and in keeping with the work on the ideological dimension of mobility (Cresswell, 2006, 2010; Endres, Manderscheid, & Mincke, 2016), we propose to differentiate four intermediate ideological positions. The latter can be broken down into positions that are more or less favorable or unfavorable to reversible mobility, depending on whether it involves the movement and migration of people, goods or capital.

The *liberal* position defends reversible mobility (both tangible and intangible) while placing limits on irreversible human mobility. In this perspective, mobility is generally considered an asset with limits, notably for security reasons. This vision reflects that of EU institutions, with more or less technical limits regarding the free movement of people, while other mobility is largely liberalized.

The proponents of a *selective position* are those with a liberal stance on tangible and intangible mobility. However, they are less liberal regarding the mobility of people. Thus, it is not merely a question of filtering migratory flows from a quantitative standpoint, but also a qualitative one. Managing immigration is a particularly sensitive issue in this sense. Reversible mobility, like that of frontier workers, may therefore also be subject to limitation and selection.

The third, the *regulatory* position, is generally favorable to human mobility but aims to apply certain limits to the mobility of objects and capital, and to introduce measures to regulate migratory flows. For its proponents, human mobility is a principle to be defended (the right to free movement), while other types of mobility require corrective measures.

The last intermediate position, the *localist* position, is characterized by the defense of proximity. In this case, territorial stability and balance are not to be jeopardized by tangible or intangible mobility flows. Human mobility is considered an asset, but only when associated with local rooting. Irreversible mobility linked to long-term migratory flows is valued rather than generalized and constant reversible mobility. Proponents of this position generally consider slow modes of transport and adaptation of the living environment an asset.

Tension clearly emerges between the norm of reversible mobility as imposed in contemporary societies and the more nuanced ideological positions that prevail in political debates on these issues in Europe. A critique of the unilateral promotion of the reversible mobility of people, goods and capital clearly emerges from these analyses.

Conclusion

Chapter 2 explored the notions of mobility and motility. Based upon this analysis, we proposed a framework for analysing political ideologies relative to the different types of mobility. Starting from the observation that European construction can be considered a mobility project in that it promotes flows, it explores the different facets of the mobility concept, i.e. mobility as a social phenomenon, mobility as an analytical indicator and finally mobility as a social norm. An examination of the relationships between these three facets allowed us to identify a gradual shift from policies of freedom of movement to policies aimed at promoting rapid, distant and frequent, reversible mobilities. In concrete terms, this shift is reflected in the fact that the aptitude for reversible mobility is becoming an increasingly central resource for social and professional integration and is gradually disqualifying other forms of mobility. The concept of motility, which was defined as a specific set of characteristics that allows an actor to be mobile or not, is useful for investigating the political dimension of mobility. Based on this understanding, mobility is a critical resource that is increasingly subject to political competition and struggle. This analytical framework based on the politics of mobility sheds new light on ideological positions regarding free movement. The political challenge, therefore, is often not unilaterally supporting or opposing free movement and mobility, but rather identifying the forms of mobility we wish to encourage.

References

Andreotti, A., Le Galès, P., & Moreno Fuentes, F. J. (2015). *Globalised minds, roots in the city: Urban upper-middle classes in Europe*. Chichester: Wiley Blackwell.

Bærenholdt, J. O. (2013). Governmobility: The powers of mobility. *Mobilities*, *8*, 20–34.

Balibar, E. (2003). *We, the people of Europe?: Reflections on transnational citizenship* (J. Swenson, Trans.). Princeton: Princeton University Press.

Bassand, M., & Brulhardt, M.-C. (1980). *Mobilité spatiale: Bilan et analyse des recherches en Suisse*. Saint-Saphorin: Georgi.

Bauman, Z. (2000). *Liquid modernity*. Cambridge, UK: Polity Press.

Boltanski, L., & Chiapello, E. (1999). *Le nouvel esprit du capitalisme*. Paris: Gallimard.

Bourdieu, P. (1986). The forms of capital. In J. Richardson (Ed.), *Handbook of theory and research for the sociology of education* (pp. 241–258). Westport: Greenwood Press.

Bourdieu, P. (2018). Social Space and the Genesis of Appropriated Physical Space. *International Journal of Urban and Regional Research*, *42*(1), 106–114.

Castells, M. (1996). *The rise of the network society*. Malden, MA: Blackwell Publishers.

Cresswell, T. (2006). *On the move: Mobility in the modern Western world*. New York: Routledge.

Cresswell, T. (2010). Towards a politics of mobility. *Environment and Planning D: Society and Space*, *28*, 17–31.

Cuin, C.-H. (1993). *Les sociologues et la mobilité sociale* (1re éd). Paris: Presses universitaires de France.

Delanty, G., & Rumford, C. (2005). *Rethinking Europe: Social theory and the implications of europeanization*. London: Routledge.

Drevon, G., Gwiazdzinski, L., & Kaufmann, V. (2019). *Proposition pour une rythmologie de la mobilité et des sociétés contemporaines*. Neuchâtel: Éditions Alphil-Presses universitaires suisses.

Durand, F., Decoville, A., & Knippschild, R. (2020). Everything all right at the internal EU borders? The ambivalent effects of cross-border integration and the rise of Euroscepticism. *Geopolitics*, *25*, 587–608.

Dürrschmidt, J. (2006). So near yet so far: Blocked networks, global links and multiple exclusion in the German–Polish borderlands. *Global Networks*, *6*, 245–263.

Endres, M., Manderscheid, K., & Mincke, C. (2016). *The mobilities paradigm: Discourses and ideologies*. London: Routledge.

Favell, A. (2008). *Eurostars and Eurocities: Free movement and mobility in an integrating Europe*. Malden: Blackwell Pub.

Fligstein, N. (2008). *Euroclash: The EU, European identity, and the future of Europe*. Oxford: Oxford University Press.

Foucault, M. (2007). *Security, territory, population: Lectures at the Collège de France, 1977–78*. Basingstoke: Palgrave Macmillan.

Gallez, C. (2015). *La mobilité quotidienne en politique. Des manières de voir et d'agir. Dossier d'habilitation à diriger des recherches Université Paris-Est Marne-la-Vallée Spécialité aménagement. Science politique*. Paris: (Université Paris-Est). Université Paris-Est.

Gallez, C., & Kaufmann, V. (2009). Aux racines de la mobilité en sciences sociales: Contribution au cadre d'analyse socio-historique de la mobilité urbaine. In V. Guigueno & M. Flonneau (Eds.), *De l'histoire des transports à l'histoire de la mobilité* (pp. 41–55). Rennes: Presses Universitaires de Rennes.

Gay, C., Kaufmann, V., & Landriève, S. (2021). *Mobilités en transition: De la norme à l'injonction*. La Tour d'Aigues: Éditions de l'Aube.

Graham, S., & Marvin, S. (2001). *Splintering urbanism: Networked infrastructures, technological mobilities and the urban condition*. London: Routledge.

Jensen, A. (2011). Mobility, space and power: On the multiplicities of seeing mobility. *Mobilities, 6*, 255–271.

Jensen, A., & Richardson, T. (2007). New region, new story: Imagining mobile subjects in transnational space. *Space and Polity, 11*, 137–150.

Jensen, O. B. (2006). 'Facework', flow and the city: Simmel, Goffman, and mobility in the contemporary city. *Mobilities, 1*, 143–165.

Jensen, O. B., & Richardson, T. (2004). *Making European space: Mobility, power and territorial identity*. London: Routledge.

Kaufmann, V. (2011). *Rethinking the city: Urban dynamics and motility*. Lausanne: Routledge; EPFL Press.

Kellerman, A. (2006). *Personal mobilities*. New York: Taylor & Francis.

Kesselring, S. (2006). Pioneering mobilities: New patterns of movement and motility in a mobile world. *Environment and Planning A: Economy and Space, 38*, 269–279.

Kuhn, T. (2011). Europa ante portas: Border residence, transnational interaction and Euroscepticism in Germany and France. *European Union Politics, 13*, 94–117.

Kuhn, T. (2015). *Experiencing European Integration: Transnational Lives and European Identity*. Oxford: Oxford University Press.

Le Breton, É. (2005). *Bouger pour s'en sortir: Mobilité quotidienne et intégration sociale*. Paris: Armand Colin.

Mau, S. (2012). *Social transnationalism: Lifeworlds beyond the nation-state* (1. issued in paperback). London: Routledge.

Merriman, P. (2012). *Mobility, space, and culture* (1st ed.). London: Routledge.

Mincke, C., & Kaufmann, V. (2017). Mobilités changeantes, mobilités intriquées. *EspacesTemps.Net Electronic Journal of Humanities and Social Sciences*. Retrieved from www.espacestemps.net/en/articles/mobilites-changeantes-mobilites-intriquees/

Mincke, C., & Montulet, B. (2019). *La société sans répit: La mobilité comme injonction*. Paris: Editions de la Sorbonne.

Montulet, B. (1998). *Les Enjeux Spatio-Temporels du Social: Mobilités*. Paris: L'Harmattan.

Newman, D. (2006). Borders and bordering: Towards an interdisciplinary dialogue. *European Journal of Social Theory, 9*, 171–186.

Nowicka, M. (2006). *Transnational professionals and their cosmopolitan universes*. Frankfurt: Campus verl.

Oosterlynck, S., & Swyngedouw, E. (2010). Noise reduction: The postpolitical quandary of night flights at Brussels airport. *Environment and Planning A, 42*, 1577–1594.

Ravalet, E., Vincent-Geslin, S., Kaufmann, V., Viry, G., & Dubois, Y. (2015). *Grandes mobilités liées au travail: Perspective européenne*. Paris: Economica.

Recchi, E. (2015). *Mobile Europe: The theory and practice of free movement in the EU*. Basingstoke: Palgrave Macmillan.

Recchi, E. (2019). Is social transnationalism fusing European societies into one? In E. Recchi, A. Favell, F. Apaydin, R. Barbulescu, M. Braun, I. Ciornei, . . . A. Varela (Eds.), *Everyday Europe: Social transnationalism in an unsettled continent* (1st ed., pp. 255–290). Bristol: Policy Press.

Recchi, E., Favell, A., Apaydin, F., Barbulescu, R., Braun, M., Ciornei, I., . . . Varela, A. (Eds.). (2019). *Everyday Europe: Social transnationalism in an unsettled continent*. Bristol: Policy Press.

Rumford, C. (2006). Theorizing borders. *European Journal of Social Theory, 9*, 155–169.

Sheller, M. (2011). Mobility. *Sociopedia.Isa*. https://doi.org/10.1177/205684601163

Sheller, M., & Urry, J. (2006). The new mobilities paradigm. *Environment and Planning A, 38*, 207–226.

Söderström, O., & Crot, L. (2010). *The mobile constitution of the society: Rethinking the mobility society nexus*. Neuchatel: Maison d'analyse de processus sociaux.

Söderström, O., Ruedin, D., Randeria, S., D'Amato, G., & Panese, F. (2013). *Critical mobilities*. Lausanne: Routledge.

Swyngedouw, E. (1993). Communication, Mobility and the Struggle for Power over Space. In G. Giannopoulos (Ed.), *Transport and Communications Innovation in Europe* (pp. 305–325). London: Belhaven Press.

Urry, J. (2007). *Mobilities*. Cambridge, UK: Polity Press.

Van Houtum, H., & Van Naerssen, T. (2002). Bordering, ordering and othering. *Tijdschrift Voor Economische En Sociale Geografie, 93*, 125–136.

Viry, G., & Kaufmann, V. (Eds.). (2015). *High mobility in Europe: Work and personal life*. Houndmills, Basingstoke Hampshire: Palgrave Macmillan.

Wright, E. O., Costello, C., Hachen, D., & Sprague, J. (1982). The American class structure. *American Sociological Review, 47*, 709–726.

3

CONSTRUCTING EUROPE THROUGH MOBILITY

Introduction

That the construction of Europe has advanced through the promotion of different types of mobility is not merely an abstract idea. On the contrary, this tendency has inspired many concrete policy interventions that have been implemented with varying degrees of success over the past decades. Participation in and acceptance of these interventions, which were designed and developed by the European authorities, depends on the different Member States concerned by these measures.

This chapter attempts to analytically summarize a set of policy measures that aim to promote different mobility flows in Europe. What types of measures have been adopted at the European level? In what policy areas and in which contexts?

EU measures to promote mobility are extremely diverse in nature. Nonetheless, it is possible to identify three main categories:

Measures to regulate the mobility framework. This first type aims to develop a common regulatory framework in order to harmonize the technical and legal conditions relating to different mobility flows. One of the founding concepts of Europe was to create a single space allowing for four types of circulation – the "four freedoms" – namely, the free movement of goods, capital, services and people within the EU.

Measures to equip and organize Europe from an infrastructural and spatial planning standpoint. This second type aims to transform Europe's geography in order to maximize the mobility conditions of the different territories and populations.

Measures aimed at encouraging and stimulating individual mobility. This third type seeks to encourage mobility by providing material and intellectual resources so that actors can meet the possible costs and difficulties associated with becoming mobile.

In reality, the three categories of measures for promoting mobility often co-exist and work conjointly. For example, the development of physical infrastructure is an

DOI: 10.4324/9780429325014-3

object of "regulation" or "incentive" in terms of its use. Measures aim not only at ensuring favorable conditions of access by acting on EU citizens' right to mobility but are often much more ambitious in scope by aiming to develop mobility knowledge and skills at the European level and to stimulate mobility projects for the inhabitants of European countries. Therefore, it is not merely a question of making mobility possible, but also of promoting it.

The Free Movement of Goods, Capital, Services and People

A Market of Mobilities

The "four freedoms" – the movement of goods, capital, services and people – form the core of the European integration project. These freedoms, together with the agriculture and transport sectors, are the cornerstone of the treaty that forged the European Economic Community (EEC) in 1957. Creating an integrated common economic area was not just one of the EU's strategic objectives; it was the privileged strategy for advancing the integration process. The treaty's establishment of a common market was the first step in this process.

To this end, the treaty provided for "the elimination, as between Member States, of customs duties and of quantitative restrictions on the import and export of goods" (art. 3a), the "establishment of a common customs tariff and of a common commercial policy towards third countries" (art. 3b), and "the abolition, as between Member States, of obstacles to freedom of movement for persons, services and capital" (art. 3c). It established that the Community should seek to promote "freedom of movement for workers" (art. 48), which was defined as the right to "move freely" (art. 48 3b), "stay" (art. 48 3c) and "remain" (art. 48 3b) in a Member State, along with the "right of establishment," allowing individuals to "take up and pursue activities as self-employed persons and to set up and manage undertakings" (art. 52). It also addresses restrictions "on freedom to provide services" (art. 59) and "on the movement of capital" (art. 67).

Since that time, European-level measures have influenced economic activity, trade, investments and the mobility of people. In 1968, customs duties on merchandise were abolished between member countries. The adoption of the Single European Act in 1986 and legislative reform to create a common market in the years that followed marked a major change. The Single European Act notably aimed to create an internal market that would serve as an "area without internal frontiers and in which the free movement of goods, persons, services and capital is ensured" (art. 26 2). The goal was to facilitate the mobility of factors of production (Majone, 2009). The link between European integration, economic integration and mobility regulation was directly observed by certain analysts (Favell & Hansen, 2002, p. 585):

> European integration is built on the growing encouragement of cross-border mobility of all kinds – canonically the free movement of capital, goods,

> services and persons – and the giving up of state sovereignty over these processes in deference to the needs of an integrated market. . . . Through the economic integration governed by the European integration process, the European nation-state's supreme early-twentieth-century control over migration and population dynamics was being voluntarily dislodged.

Despite these efforts, economic integration has not been fully achieved, and many barriers remain between the different European Member States. While the complete mobility of capital has seemingly been accomplished, the mobility of goods and services appears to be more limited due to legal and technical barriers, and/or consumer habits. The mobility of people and that of workers more specifically is thought to be much more limited due to cultural and linguistic differences between European countries.

Similarly, the positive correlation between the creation of the euro and the increase in the mobility of other factors of production is far from being proven. According to Krugman (Krugman, 2013), three economic arguments seem to justify the adoption of a single currency: the benefits of monetary integration for trade in goods and services; the fact that monetary autonomy is no longer necessary when workers can move to where the jobs are located, and; the creation of common budgets to benefit from a single monetary policy. From the economic crisis of the late 2000s, Krugman concludes that the first two arguments are insufficient to ensure the proper functioning of a common monetary area. He and other observers (Farole, Rodríguez-Pose, & Storper, 2011) caution against the risk of economic adjustment through labor mobility, which could lead to the economic and fiscal weakening of labor-exporting countries. Some observers consider that in many regions, the process of European integration has reinforced deindustrialization and brain drain phenomena, leading to intergenerational unemployment, poverty, social exclusion and demographic decline (Dühr, Colomb, & Nadin, 2010).

An Area Without Borders

Yet, as Recchi (2015, pp. 2–3) points out, human mobility in Europe cannot be just considered as a mere component of the single market:

> Making it a component of the single market, however, does not do justice to the legal and practical implications of the EU free movement regime. Its significance is decidedly broader, for people are not merely producers and consumers. Freedom of movement in the EU alters the traditional notion of national citizenship, which is intrinsically both a privilege and a spatial constraint.

By tracing the history of the right to free movement in Europe, Recchi shows how the content, the categories of persons concerned and the spatial scope of the right to free movement have changed considerably over time. The mobility of European inhabitants has thus become the crux of the notion of European citizenship. The right to free movement and residence across the EU territory is indeed the "true keystone of the edifice of European citizenship" (2015, p. 27). As a result of this development, the "migrant workers" of the Member States of the past are now European "mobile persons."

The idea of an area without borders culminated in 1990 with the Schengen agreements. The truck drivers' strike that paralyzed European borders in the spring of 1984 sparked reactions by certain national governments. France and Germany were the precursors of a single mobility area project, which envisaged the gradual abolition of controls at the borders of these two countries. Belgium, the Netherlands and Luxembourg took interest soon thereafter. Five years later, the five countries signed the Schengen Convention. This Convention distinguished between "internal borders," which are "the common land borders of the Contracting Parties, their airports for internal flights and their seaports for regular ferry connections exclusively from or to other ports within the territories of the Contracting Parties," (art. 1) and "external borders," which are "the remainder of the land and sea boundaries, as well as airports and seaports of the Contracting Parties." The Convention also defined how traffic at external borders would be subject to the control of the competent authorities and aimed to eliminate controls of individuals at internal borders, while ensuring internal security and controlling migratory flows.

With the entry into force of the Amsterdam Treaty, the Schengen acquis was incorporated into the EU framework. In the first decade of the 2000s, various measures were adopted, such as the creation of a European Agency for the Management of Operational Cooperation at the External Borders (FRONTEX); an External Borders Fund to assist certain Member States that bore a heavier burden in terms of the control of persons and border surveillance due to their geographic location; and the European Border Surveillance System (EUROSUR) for detecting, preventing and combating illegal immigration and cross-border crime. The European neighborhood policy that was implemented in the mid-1990s clearly aims to strengthen the control of external borders. Some observers conclude that Schengen has gone from a project combining "freedom of movement" and "security" to one focused mainly on security issues (Zaiotti, 2011).

This shift has been criticized by some. Walters, for instance, considers that Europe's illegal immigration policy is fundamentally aimed at isolating the territory and treats Europe as an autonomous region/entity, distinct from and in opposition to other delimited entities (Walters, 2008). For such observers, "Schengenland" has turned Europe into "a home that must be protected from those who don't live in it, who may enter as guests, but should have no claim to stay there permanently" (Walters & Haahr, 2005, p. 139). Indeed, in the aftermath of the September 11th attacks, Europe's borders remained blurred and permeable and migration flows were defined and governed by economic factors (Favell & Hansen, 2002). Soon thereafter, however, its policy toughened though selectively. Favell noted the contradiction between the porosity to the east (through a policy of enlargement) and hardening of borders to the south (Favell, 2009).

This brief overview of measures in terms of mobility regulation within Europe highlights a "loss of boundary control" at the national level (Scharpf, 1998, p. 16) in favor of market integration and the creation of a space of mobility. For its designers, market integration requires the elimination of all obstacles, restrictions, limitations and barriers to mobility. At the same time, new common rules are being adopted. These regulatory measures aim to create a space of "perfect mobility," to better ensure Europe's economic and political integration.

Equipping the Continent

The simple right to free movement does not naturally result in an increase in actual mobility. For there to be mobility, this right must be put into practice through the creation of physical infrastructures. This mechanistic concept of supply has guided interventions at European level in terms of investment in large transport infrastructure. In this section, we will outline the major measures taken in this area.

Trans-European Networks

The Trans-European Networks (TENs) program is the most ambitious intervention in terms of infrastructure supply at the European level. The TENs program has been part of the European treaties since its inclusion in the Maastricht Treaty in 1992. Despite the many difficulties linked to its implementation, and to financial constraints most notably, the TENs program remains on the EU's agenda today. Title XII of the Maastricht Treaty (art. 129b) is explicit in the objectives, namely to:

> enable citizens of the Union, economic operators and regional and local communities to derive full benefit from the setting up of an area without internal frontiers, the Community shall contribute to the establishment and development of trans-European networks in the areas of transport, telecommunications and energy infrastructures.
>
> *(Council of the European Communities, 1992)*

Three principles of the TENs program are closely linked: the creation and/or modernization of infrastructures, technological standardization and the liberalization of the market. While large infrastructures have traditionally been developed for national territories, the TENs program aims to tackle infrastructure planning at the European level.

The TEN-Transport (TEN-T) program plays a very important symbolic role in the strategy of European networks. This is most likely due to the spatial visualization of these infrastructures through images and maps, and their impact on and physical presence in the territory. The TEN-T includes infrastructures for land (road, rail, inland waterways), air, sea and multimodal transport. As defined currently, the TEN-T includes a "global network" comprised of more than 130,000 km of railways and roads and a "core network" consisting of those parts of the global network with the greatest strategic importance.

Some observers consider that the TEN-T program "strengthens" the discourse on market and political integration (Jensen & Richardson, 2004), creating new mobility potential within Europe and the surrounding territories. Other observers cite the possible contradiction between the objectives of cohesion and territorial balance within the EU and the dynamics of spatial concentration linked to such a large infrastructure (Dühr et al., 2010). The development of large infrastructures can in fact reinforce dynamics of differentiation between central and peripheral areas in Europe, and between urban centers and rural areas.

The TEN-Transport is a fundamental part of the common transport policy to ensure mobility potential in the European territory. Improving mobility conditions remains a strategic objective in this area, whereas other perspectives such as modal shifts and environmental impact have only been included more recently. It was not until the early 2000s and the publishing of the white paper "European transport policy for 2010: time to decide" that the possibility of controlling or slowing down the development of mobility made its way onto the agenda. The white paper proposed "the option of gradually breaking the link between economic growth and transport growth" without restricting the mobility of people and goods. This strategy was eventually abandoned. In 2011, the new white paper "Roadmap to a Single European Transport Area – Towards a competitive and resource efficient transport system" explicitly states that curbing mobility is not an option.

The Single European Sky

Even if it is not labeled a TEN-T project, the Single European Sky initiative has a strong regulatory character that has allowed for major developments in air traffic. The organization of air transport in Europe has undergone significant changes since the 1980s. By the end of that decade, domestic air markets, previously under the control of governments and public airlines, were opened up to competition. Any European airline with a technical certification can now offer national or international routes within Europe.

Launched in the late 1990s, the Single European Sky initiative aims to increase transport capacity and to ensure aviation safety through the development of an integrated air traffic control system. In 1999, the European Commission (European Commission, 1999) considered that:

> Europe cannot keep the frontiers in the sky that it has managed to eliminate on the ground; it must allow the freedom of movement of persons, goods and services beyond such frontiers.

The Single European Sky was implemented in stages. In 2004, three regulations relating to the provision of air navigation services, organization, use of airspace and interoperability of the European air transport management network were adopted. Starting in 2009, new legislative initiatives emerged to increase the economic performance of the regulatory framework, given the increase in the demand and potential insufficiency of the infrastructure's capacity.

While the territorial footprint of this initiative is limited compared to other TEN infrastructure projects, the reorganization of the aviation sector in Europe is seemingly driven by the same logic of improving mobility potential while neutralizing the adverse effects in terms of safety or environmental issues (Jensen & Richardson, 2004).

Regional Policy

Since the late 1980s, regional policy has been a key investment policy at the European level, representing around 0.4% of the EU's GDP. While the Treaty of Rome established harmonious development as one of the Community's tasks, it was not until 1975 and the creation of the European Regional Development Fund (ERDF) that regional policy truly underpinned a first development project (Drevet, 2008). Over the next decades, the ERDF financed many projects in Europe's poorest regions in order to rebalance the European territory.

With the integration of Greece, Spain and Portugal in the 1980s, regional policy gained momentum. The Delors Commission aimed to create a synergy by mitigating both disparities and barriers to free movement (Drevet, 2008). To this end, a common framework was forged for the various structural funds, and their budget was doubled. In 1992 the Cohesion Fund was set up to offset the efforts of the most disadvantaged Member States in order to meet convergence criteria for the adoption of a single currency. This new fund helped finance projects in the field of environmental and transport infrastructure, notably those of the TEN-T. In addition, specific programs were developed regionally to ensure development in specific areas such as border regions (with the European Territorial Cooperation (better known as INTERREG) program) and peripheral regions (with the REGIS program). Finally, during the 1990s and 2000s, pre-accession instruments, such as the Instrument for Structural Policies for Pre-Accession (ISPA), were also created as part of regional policies.

Regional policy aims to promote balanced development of the European territory in terms of competitiveness, sustainable development and governance. It is also a strategy for limiting internal migration within the European territory (Drevet, 2008, p. 263):

> While growth does not provide sufficient jobs to reduce unemployment rates, recent developments have helped create enough jobs in areas formerly condemned to emigration to reverse this trend. In a Europe where political and linguistic fragmentation greatly limits the mobility of the workforce

> compared to other major areas, such as China or the United States, this is essential. Since this mobility cannot be greatly increased within the EU, it is imperative that the distribution of jobs approximate that of the population geographically speaking, which is inconceivable without a policy that pursues this objective explicitly.

In practice, regional policy has contributed to rebalancing the territory from the standpoint of differences between the Member States, while interregional inequalities within States seem to have increased (Faludi, 2010). Some analysts highlight tensions between territorial cohesion objectives and intra-regional competitiveness strategies, which have become widespread in recent decades in Europe and beyond (Tewdwr-Jones, 2011). Others consider that spatial planning policies actually increase the mobility potential of European citizens. While opposing the idea of promoting mobility as a priority option, the Barca report on regional policy reform stressed that mobility opportunities must be part of the EU's policy (Barca, 2009, p. 37):

> The second misconception is that place-based development policies restrict mobility by encouraging people not to move from places. On the contrary, the virtue of the policy is that it broadens people's opportunities and gives them more substantive freedom in choosing whether or not to move. If place-based development policies were about reducing mobility, they would be against efficiency and equity, since the option of moving is an important ingredient in both. On the contrary, place-based policies are, in fact, intended to enhance individuals' substantive freedom in deciding whether to stay (and to make the most of staying) or to move (and to make the most of moving).

In the same perspective as that of the Barca report, initiatives developed within the regional policy framework have focused mainly on the question of mobility. This is the case for the territorial cooperation program INTERREG, which financed many projects. Certain issues, such as pollution and transport infrastructure, have been priorities for territorial cooperation (Dühr et al., 2010). Transport infrastructure and mobility programs (students, researchers, etc.) play a key role in territorial cooperation, like in the Øresund, the Alpine space, and cooperation between France and Spain along the Pyrenees.

Strategy for the Development of the European Territory

While thinking on spatial planning has been done at the European level within the framework of regional policy, early initiatives regarding this issue originated elsewhere within the Council of Europe, with the creation of the latter's Conference of Ministers Responsible for Spatial/Regional Planning (CEMAT) in 1970.

It was within the CEMAT that the Charter of Torremolinos, for instance, which is considered the first planning document at the European level, was drawn up and adopted in 1983. This Charter addresses a series of recommendations to European institutions. It states that (COE, 1983):

> Regional/spatial planning is an important instrument in the evolution of European society and that the intensification of international co-operation in this field represents a substantial contribution towards a stronger European identity.

During the 1990s, European institutions attempted to favor a European perspective in the area of spatial planning more systematically under the technical guidance of the Spatial Development Committee (CDS), which was established in 1991. This strategy led to the adoption of the European Spatial Development Perspective (ESDP) in 1999. The ESDP identified a single, large, globally influential geographical area of economic integration in a geographical perimeter that includes London, Paris, Milan, Munich and Hamburg. This area accounts for 20% of the EU's surface, 40% of its population and contributes roughly 50% of Europe's GDP. Given this concentration, the ESDP advocated for a polycentric approach to territorial development in order to create several areas of global economic integration. In terms of mobility, the ESDP noted that the mobility of people, goods and information in the EU was characterized by concentration and polarization tendencies. Consequently, the ESDP considered that all regions should have adequate access to infrastructure, while ensuring that the creation of high-quality infrastructure neither reduced resources in structurally weaker peripheral regions (pump effect), nor crossed them without connecting them (tunnel effect).

Some observers pointed out that the ESDP's role remains ambiguous insofar as its discourse in favor of territorial competitiveness prevails over the rebalancing strategy argument (Dühr et al., 2010). While the ESDP has not been directly implemented, its development has been an important learning and pooling experience at the European level (Faludi, 2010). It was based on this document, for instance, that the European Observation Network, Territorial Development and Cohesion (ESPON) was created in 2002 to carry out studies on planning and territorial strategy at the European level.

This development in spatial planning contributed to the Treaty of Lisbon adding a territorial dimension to the objectives of EU economic and social cohesion. It was in this context that the Commission presented the "Green Paper on Territorial Cohesion: turning territorial diversity into strength" in 2008. This document stressed the need to work towards the "harmonious development of all of these territories" by focusing on concentration, connectivity and cooperation. In 2011, EU Planning Ministers drafted a document that cited the objectives of territorial rebalancing and harmonious development. This document (EU Ministers Responsible for Spatial Planning and Territorial Development, 2011, pp. 4–7) stressed the need to improve connectivity across Europe:

> The growing interdependence of regions generates a demand for better connectivity at global, European and national levels. Integration barriers at the local and regional level can result in the underutilization of human, cultural, economic and ecological resources in border regions and increase their peripheral position and, hence, social exclusion. . . . We believe that fair and affordable accessibility to services of general interest, information, knowledge and mobility are essential for territorial cohesion. Providing services and minimizing infrastructure barriers can improve competitiveness and the sustainable and harmonious territorial development of the EU.

Support for Urban Policies

Since the 1990s, the urban dimension has also attracted the interest of European institutions with a view to increasing trade and improving interconnectivity. Between 1988 and 2006, it was notably through the URBAN programs that Europe carried out interventions at the urban level. These programs sought to develop an integrated approach to addressing urban issues. This field of action was strengthened in the 2000s with the development of the "Leipzig Charter on Sustainable European Cities." This charter aimed to promote integrated urban development in a sustainable way, calling for measures to ensure the circulation and interconnectivity of urban areas. Similarly, the "Cities of Tomorrow" document (European Commission, 2011), which identified the European model of sustainable urban development, emphasizes inter-city connectivity as central for urban development:

> The connectivity of Europe's cities is a key element in creating balanced territorial development. Many European cities benefit from good connectivity by air or rail with other major European cities, allowing for business day trips with full-day meeting possibilities. Such cities have good 'contactability'.

Unlike urban spaces, rural areas seem by and large to fall outside European policies' strategy of mobility and territorial connectivity. The Common Agricultural Policy (CAP) is fundamentally characterized by its focus on protecting indigenous agricultural production. The CAP could be considered a stabilizing intervention at the territorial level. However, studies on the territorial impact of this policy have found that the CAP has acted contrary to the ESDP's objective of balanced territorial development and has not supported its objectives of economic and social cohesion in its favoring of central EU areas and those most accessible from a local standpoint (ESPON, 2006). Similarly, some observers consider that the CAP has done little to prevent the loss of jobs in the agricultural sector, the depopulation of rural areas and rural flight (Dühr et al., 2010).

The different types of interventions we have just described must be seen as part of the EU's general strategy for improving the material conditions of mobility. Through the creation of infrastructure and spatial planning, the goal has been to promote the mobility of economic actors and inhabitants across the European territory.

Making Actors Motile and Inciting Them to Be Mobile

A regulatory framework and the creation of facilities and physical infrastructure are not the only ways in which Europe has promoted mobility. To address the difficulties individuals face in order to become mobile, it has also developed measures to support them in their mobility strategies.

This third area of intervention concerns motility in general. The term motility (Kaufmann, Bergman, & Joye, 2004) refers to the enabling of mobility through access (the right to mobility and ability to use mobility equipment) and development of the necessary knowledge and skills to incorporate mobility into individuals' lives (desire to move). The message is clear: mobility must not remain dormant but, on the contrary, must be activated. Let us look at some of the incentives that Europe has provided in this area.

The European Social Fund

Incentives with regard to mobility notably concern the areas of employment and training. A flagship initiative in this area was the European Social Fund (ESF), which was the first structural fund to improve job mobility within the EU. The ESF was provided for in the Treaty of Rome:

> In order to improve opportunities of employment of workers in the Common Market and thus contribute to raising the standard of living, a European Social Fund shall hereby be established in accordance with the provisions set out below; it shall have the task of promoting within the Community employment facilities and the geographical and occupational mobility of workers.
>
> *(European Economic Community, 1957)*

The ESF has been used extensively to finance youth exchange programs, whose aim is to forge European awareness in the form of apprenticeships. Initially, the ESF was designed for workers in southern Italy and used as a compensation fund for the costs imposed on the Member States due to problems of geographical mobility of workers from regions with high unemployment (Leboutte, 2008). One of the ESF's key roles at that time was to encourage unemployed persons to move within the Community in order to seek jobs. It was workers – as a factor of production – and not citizens of Member Countries who had the right to move freely within the framework of the ESF.

The ESF was reformed several times in the decades that followed. Although originally conceived as an instrument of proactive employment policy from the 1980s onwards, it became a system of social cohesion and territorial redistribution with its rapprochement to other structural funds (Brine, 2002). Its objectives included the integration of women and young people into the labor market through the promotion of vocational training and retraining.

Yet, mobility in this framework remains a strategic objective to improve workers' employability. In this context, during the economic crisis of the 2010s, geographical mobility became part of the ESF initiative. A document by the Commission (European Commission, 2014, p. 9) raises this question very clearly:

> The crisis has not added so much to in-country differences, but created significant cross-country labour market disparities. As a result, higher cross-border mobility becomes an important factor for improving resource allocation in order to outbalance local labour market situations across Europe. However, intra-EU mobility is still low in most EU countries despite recent improvements.

In this context, the document states that "policies to encourage workers' mobility across Europe are becoming more important if one considers the labour market outlook for the next ten years." Through the "Strengthening employment and mobility" line, the ESF is currently helping job seekers move across Europe to find work. These actions are inspired by the Europe 2020 strategy for growth and employment, in which mobility for work is a key area. More specifically, the Commission (European Commission, 2010) will endeavor to:

> facilitate and promote intra-EU labour mobility and better match labour supply with demand with appropriate financial support from the structural funds, notably the European Social Fund (ESF), and to promote a forward-looking and comprehensive labour migration policy which would respond in a flexible way to the priorities and needs of labour markets.

The strategy of encouraging mobility is particularly aimed at young people. One of the ESF's objectives is precisely to encourage mobility so that "thousands of young people gain work experience and language skills abroad" (European Commission, 2012).

ERASMUS

The European Community Action Scheme for the Mobility of University Students (ERASMUS) program is perhaps the most emblematic EU initiative in terms of mobility for learning purposes. As early as 1987, ERASMUS replaced a university cooperation action program launched in 1976. The ERASMUS program was directly inspired by the Adonino reports (Feyen, 2013), which aimed to create provisions that directly affected Community citizens, bringing tangible benefits to their everyday lives. Since 1987, through the ERASMUS program, Europe has contributed to funding student mobility by enabling almost three million students to complete their studies or do internships abroad.

The spirit of the program has also evolved over time. Initially, its main objectives were to create a European demos and to promote cultural exchange. Today, the ERASMUS program has evolved towards the acquisition of knowledge to improve students' skills in the labor market (Klose, 2013). In 1995, the ERASMUS program was integrated into the SOCRATES initiative, which was designed to help in developing quality education and training and to create an open European area of cooperation in education. The Leonardo da Vinci program was created at the same time to develop a professional training policy by, inter alia, implementing transnational investment and exchange programs. Beginning in 2014, all of these programs were grouped together under the Erasmus+ initiative, which set out to make the mobility of "individuals for education and training purposes" its main goal by supporting the implementation of mobility projects in the areas of education, training and youth.

Democratizing Mobility

In the early 2000s, mobility emerged as the essential goal of the European integration project, when the European Council of Nice approved its resolution on a "mobility action plan." Member States must commit:

> to meet[ing] the great expectations of their fellow citizens that, with the support of the Commission, each in its field and in full compliance with the principle of subsidiarity, it will take the steps necessary to remove obstacles to mobility and to promote it.
>
> *(European Council, 2000)*

An action plan aimed at defining and democratizing mobility in Europe was proposed to promote adequate financing and to increase mobility. The plan lays out 42 measures with regard to the training of persons, financing mobility, improving mobility and enhancing mobility periods. Consequently, in 2001, the Commission published a brochure for young Europeans entitled "Passport to mobility: learning differently, learning abroad" (European Commission, 2001). This document, which states that "moving with the times means embracing cross-frontier mobility," that "mobility is everyone's business" and advocates for "lifelong mobility," posits that "the next stage is to make mobility as widely accessible as possible." Among other things, this document announced the development of a CV model known as Europass, which was designed to facilitate job-related mobility both between countries and sectors.

This strategy continued in the 2000s with the creation of a "High Level Expert Forum on Mobility," whose mandate in 2008 was to expand mobility not only within the university sector but among young people more generally. Similarly, in 2009, the Commission published the "Promoting the learning mobility of young people" green paper, which discussed preparation for a period of mobility abroad. In the Europe 2020 strategy, a Youth on the Move initiative was launched to encourage them to take advantage of European scholarships to study or train in another country. In these circumstances, one can deduce that young Europeans are to become "highly skilled workers, seeking professional added value or moving for study reasons and whose migration may only be temporary" (Murphy-Lejeune, 2002).

These mobility efforts have been particularly important in terms of academic research and university cooperation since the late 1990s. The 1999 Bologna Declaration, the cornerstone of European higher education, established a credit system as a means of promoting student mobility as widely as possible. Simultaneously, during the 2000s, efforts were made to strengthen the European Research Area through programs supporting the mobility of researchers, such as the Marie Skłodowska-Curie Actions.

Conclusion

All of these initiatives, which nonetheless are an institutional injunction to mobility, aim explicitly to encourage "mobility." Far from being disconnected from or independent of one another, they converge in a common agenda in which mobility is a key strategic element. While the actual effects of the measures adopted are most likely not commensurate with their initial ambitions, this action program is becoming increasingly systematic, with mobility gradually playing a preponderant role. For certain populations such as young people, unemployed persons and researchers, this observation goes even further, with mobility as the miracle solution to their respective problems.

The conception of the EU as a project to promote mobility is not independent of the dynamics of generalization and intensification of global mobility flows. Deregulation, regionalization and economic globalization measures, which have increased since the 1980s, have given rise to new types of mobility. However, in no other model of economic integration or cooperation does mobility seem to have played such a relevant political role as in the case of the EU. In short, while the mobility phenomenon is concomitant with the globalization process, Europe has pushed further its political value and significance.

In any case, it seems clear that the European integration model based on promoting mobility has reached its limit. On the one hand, mobility, it would seem, does not succeed in guaranteeing territorial integration for Europe through supranational solidarities and a common citizenship/identity. The functionalist approach that inspired the European project is currently being questioned. On the other hand, mobility in itself cannot be regarded as a factor of adjustment and regulation that maximizes the opportunities of economic actors and European citizens with regard to the development of a single market. More notably, the free movement of persons alone seemingly does not ensure the integration of European workers and unemployed people. It is difficult as such to consider social integration based on the promotion of mobility as a systematically applied strategy. Finally, based on this diagnosis, the forces opposed to the process of European integration have put the principle of free movement – particularly with regard to the mobility of people – in the spotlight. These perspectives advocate for a return to and reestablishment of national borders.

References

Barca, F. (Ed.). (2009). An agenda for a reformed cohesion policy – A place-based approach to meeting European Union challenges and expectations. Brussels: European Communities.

Brine, J. (2002). *The European social fund and the EU: Flexibility, growth, stability*. London: Sheffield Academic Press.

COE, C. of E. (1983). *European regional/spatial planning Charter Torremolinos Charter*. Brussels: Council of Europe.

Council of the European Communities (Ed.). (1992). *Treaty on European Union*. Luxembourg: Office for Official Publications of the European Communities.

Drevet, J.-F. (2008). *Histoire de la politique régionale de l'Union européenne*. Paris: Belin.

Dühr, S., Colomb, C., & Nadin, V. (2010). *European spatial planning and territorial cooperation*. London: Routledge.

ESPON. (2006). *L'impact territorial de la PAC et de la politique de développement rural*. Luxembourg: European Spatial Planning Observation Network.

EU Ministers Responsible for Spatial Planning and Territorial Development. (2011). *Territorial agenda of the European union 2020 towards an inclusive, smart and sustainable Europe of diverse regions*. Retrieved January 15, 2021, from https://ec.europa.eu/regional_policy/sources/policy/what/territorial-cohesion/territorial_agenda_2020.pdf

European Commission. (1999). Communication from the Commission to the council and the European parliament – The creation of the single European sky /* COM/99/0614 final */. Retrieved June 27, 2016, from http://eur-lex.europa.eu/legal-content/FR/TXT/?uri=celex%3A51999DC0614

European Commission. (2001). *Passport to mobility: Learning differently: Learning abroad*. Luxembourg: Office for Official Publications of the European Communities.

European Commission. (2010). *EUROPE 2020 A strategy for smart, sustainable and inclusive growth*. Luxembourg: Publications Office of the European Union.

European Commission (Ed.). (2011). *Cities of tomorrow: Challenges, visions, ways forward* (Oct. 2011). Luxembourg: Publications Office of the European Office.

European Commission. (2012). *The European social fund: Investing in people: What it is and what it does*. Luxembourg: Publications Office of the European Union.

European Commission. (2014). *Promoting inclusive growth: European Social Fund thematic paper*. Luxembourg: Publications Office.

European Council. (2000). *Nice European Council 7-10 December 2000. Presidency conclusions and annexes*. Nice: EU European Council.

European Economic Community. (1957). *Treaty Establishing the European Economic Community and Connected Documents*. Secretariat of the Interim Committee for the Common Market and EURATOM.

Faludi, A. (2010). *Cohesion, coherence, cooperation: European spatial planning coming of age?* (1st publ). London: Routledge.

Farole, T., Rodríguez-Pose, A., & Storper, M. (2011). Cohesion policy in the European Union: Growth, geography, institutions. *JCMS: Journal of Common Market Studies, 49*, 1089–1111.

Favell, A. (2009). Immigration, migration, and free movement in the making of Europe. In *Contemporary European politics. European identity* (pp. 167–190). Cambridge: Cambridge University Press.

Favell, A., & Hansen, R. (2002). Markets against politics: Migration, EU enlargement and the idea of Europe. *Journal of Ethnic and Migration Studies, 28*, 581–601.

Feyen, B. (2013). The making of a success story: The creation of the ERASMUS programme in the historical context. In B. Feyen & E. Krzaklewska (Eds.), *The ERASMUS phenomenon: Symbol of a new European generation?* (pp. 21–38). Frankfurt am Main: Lang.

Jensen, O. B., & Richardson, T. (2004). *Making European space: Mobility, power and territorial identity*. London: Routledge.

Kaufmann, V., Bergman, M. M., & Joye, D. (2004). Motility: Mobility as capital. *International Journal of Urban and Regional Research, 28*, 745–756.

Klose, U. (2013). The making of a success story: The creation of the ERASMUS programme in the historical context. In B. Feyen & E. Krzaklewska (Eds.), *The ERASMUS phenomenon: Symbol of a new European generation?* (pp. 39–50). Frankfurt am Main: Lang.

Krugman, P. (2013). *Moneda común, destino común*. Retrieved June 24, 2016, from http://blogs.elpais.com/paul-krugman/2013/06/una-moneda-comun-un-destino-comun.html

Leboutte, R. (2008). *Histoire économique et sociale de la construction européenne*. Bruxelles: PIE Lang.

Majone, G. (2009). *Europe as the would-be world power: The EU at fifty*. Cambridge: Cambridge University Press.

Murphy-Lejeune, E. (2002). *Student mobility and narrative in Europe: The new strangers*. London: Routledge.

Recchi, E. (2015). *Mobile Europe: The theory and practice of free movement in the EU*. Basingstoke: Palgrave Macmillan.

Scharpf, F. W. (1998). Negative and positive integration in the political economy of European Welfare States. In G. Marks, F. W. Scharpf, P. C. Schmitter, & W. Steeck (Eds.), *Governance in the European Union* (Reprinted, pp. 15–39). London: Sage Publications.

Tewdwr-Jones, M. (2011). Cohesion and competitiveness: The evolving context for European territorial development. In N. Adams, G. Cotella, & R. Nunes (Eds.), *Territorial development, cohesion and spatial planning; Knowledge and policy development in an enlarged EU* (pp. 69–83). London: Routledge.

Walters, W. (2008). Anti-illegal immigration policy: The case of the European Union. In C. Gabriel & P. Hélène (Eds.), *Governing international labour migration: Current issues, challenges and dilemmas* (pp. 43–59). London: Routledge.

Walters, W., & Haahr, J. H. (2005). *Governing Europe: Discourse, governmentality and European integration*. London: Routledge.

Zaiotti, R. (2011). *Cultures of border control: Schengen and the evolution of European frontiers*. Chicago: University of Chicago Press.

4

FROM FREE MOVEMENT TO THE OBLIGATION TO BE MOBILE

Introduction

Building Europe through measures that favor free movement and are designed to promote mobility has resulted in an exponential increase in flows across the continent. This chapter looks more specifically at the different forms human mobility takes in conjunction with the development of the speed potential of rapid transport and telecommunication systems. The first part of the chapter provides an overview of certain trends in the role of travel in lifestyles. The second part focuses on work-related high mobility based on the results of the "Job Mobilities and Family Lives in Europe" research data.

Mobilities and Lifestyles in Europe

Few surveys in Europe have measured the mobility of a population for a period of a week or more. The "mobility and lifestyles" survey on the French population carried out by the Mobile Lives Forum in 2019 was an exception in this sense in that it covered all forms of travel for a sample of 13,201 people over a two-week period. It showed that, in 2019, French people traveled an average of 400 kilometers and more than 10 hours per week. However, these averages tell us little about the nature and diversity of travel practices. The survey revealed that the 10% of the French population that travels the least on a daily basis spends an average of ten minutes or less a day (about an hour a week) getting from place to place, versus nearly five hours a day (34 hours a week) for the 10% of the population that travels the most – in other words, more than 30 times more (Forum Vies Mobiles, 2020).

While this diversity is often used to explain the difficulty in building social cohesion in European and North American societies, the actual details of this diversity are rarely quantified. The Mobile Lives Forum data notably helps us understand

DOI: 10.4324/9780429325014-4

this diversity with regard to different lifestyles and the inequalities associated with them. Thus, identifying individuals' daily activities helps us to better grasp the spatial and temporal dimensions of lifestyles, and the paces and movement associated with them at different spatial and temporal scales. At the same time, measuring aspirations and attitudes towards mobility helps us identify the meaning that people ascribe it, their commitment to their mobility and the activities associated with them.

The diversity of the lifestyles observed through this data concerns the activities of daily life and their location, spatial scope and temporality; activities schedules; holiday and leisure activities; residential location choices; and the values underlying these practices and choices.

It is in this way that daily activities are either separated in time and in space or, on the contrary, are combined, in the same way that some see travel time as a time in its own right while others see it merely as an interstice between activities. Some people also seem to enjoy breaking up their day between home and a workplace several hundred kilometers apart, while others appreciate living more locally.

The survey also highlights the importance of professional activity in terms of mobility (Forum Vies Mobiles, 2020). Every week, working people spend nearly 12 hours commuting, versus only seven for non-working people, and travel nearly 500 kilometers, compared to just over 200 kilometers for the latter.

However, behind these work-related commuting data lies a plethora of practices. Given the rise in professions that demand significant travel (especially in the service sector), we must not limit our understanding of work-related mobility to travel between home and the workplace.

Job-related mobility can be broken down into three main types: 1) travel between home and the workplace, which often requires use of a means of transport; 2) business travel as part of a job (visiting customers or colleagues at other sites, or structurally mobile professions in the transportation sector); and 3) relocating to another region or abroad to change jobs within the same company or to work for a new employer.

In Europe, all three types of mobility are increasing and have led to the proliferation of new lifestyles that are largely shaped by work-related mobility:

- Home to work commutes are becoming increasingly distant and frequent due to advances in transport speeds and flexible working schedules in many professions,[1] as well as personal/residential choices wherein three to four-hour commutes are typical.
- Business travel is also increasing and now concerns not only top management and salespeople but also middle managers in large companies.
- There has been exponential growth in the number of mobile workstations with the boom in road transport and in the logistics sector (drivers, delivery people). Posted workers have joined the ranks of "mobile workers," like fairground employees and seasonal workers of yore.

Work-related mobility has, as such, given rise to new forms of travel that, until 30 years ago, were unprecedented (Le Marchand, 2011; Ravalet, Vincent-Geslin, Kaufmann, Viry, & Dubois, 2015), namely:

- different forms of weekly commuting (two or more residences in different geographical locations);
- long-distance and long-term commuting, which has led to more and more people travelling hundreds of kilometers for long hours each day to get to their place of work only to return home in the evening; and
- new forms of nomadism or itinerancy associated with mobile habitats.

An analysis of these practices reveals a complex set of compromises that represents "the least bad solution" households adopt in the face of numerous constraints.

The Mobile Lives Forum's survey also revealed that 40% of French working people are mobile for their jobs, be they mobile workers by definition, such as bus drivers and delivery people, or people who travel daily for work (repair people, in-home helpers, sales representatives, etc.) (Forum Vies Mobiles, 2020).

Conclusions on Intensely Paced Lifestyles

These figures suggest that rapid and regular work-related travel has become a valued form of travel in Europe. This valorization goes hand in hand with the "invisibilization" of travel (both time and distance) among individuals and employers alike. Companies, for instance, generally consider 1) that getting from home to work and back is the employee's personal responsibility; 2) that business trips are supposed to be "rewarding" and are poorly compensated (only employees that are considered "mobile" like drivers and delivery people are compensated for sleeping away from home); and 3) that professional mobility that involves relocating either domestically or abroad is the earmark of a successful career (Sergot, Chabault, & Loubaresse, 2012).

Nowadays, one must be willing and able to move fast, far and frequently, not only to find, keep or change jobs, but also for leisure travel such as vacations or to gain work experience abroad (Le Breton, 2005). In other words, reversible mobility has become a social norm. While this injunction concerns all spheres of activity (Mincke & Montulet, 2019), it is particularly prevalent in the work world.

This willingness to travel fast, far and frequently is a "must" for anyone who claims to be dynamic, motivated or ambitious (Ravalet, Vincent-Geslin, Kaufmann, & Leveugle, 2014; Sergot et al., 2012). Knowing how to identify and play with the rules of this injunction to mobility is thus an essential skill for social and professional integration in general, and for upward career mobility in particular. Developing forms of motility that enable one to withstand a fast-paced life has become a kind of insurance. Having access, skills and mobility projects that support lifestyles in which the intensive use of the speed potentials of rapid transport and telecommunications systems is a key resource for social and professional integration. Conversely, having limited access, skills or mobility projects that make such fast-paced, high-pressure lifestyles bearable – or willingly refusing such lifestyles – often leads to job loss, difficulty in finding a job, and even socio-professional downgrading (Kaufmann, Ravalet, & Drevon, 2020).

In other words, Europeans today are expected to have a certain type of motility that allows them to seize the opportunities afforded by policies that promote free movement, barrier-free European labor market and rapid transit with the development of road, high-speed rail and air infrastructure.

However, numerous research studies indicate that the fast-paced lifestyles that result from this injunction to mobility are exhausting and do not correspond to people's aspirations. Those who commute most intensively describe themselves as exhausted (Ravalet et al., 2014), are prone to burn-out and often struggle to reconcile their professional and private lives. This is especially true for women.

The international survey conducted by the Forum Vies Mobiles in 2015 (Forum Vies Mobiles, 2016) on lifestyle aspirations in Germany, Spain, France, Japan, Turkey and the US among a representative sample of their respective populations indicated that many people in these six countries felt the pace was tiring and wished it were slower. The data thus revealed that a slower pace of life was an aspiration for many of those surveyed:

- 74% of respondents felt the pace of life in today's society was too fast (80% in France, Germany, Spain, USA);
- 78% personally wished they could slow down (82% in France);
- 50% said that they did not have the time to do what they want or need to do.

This desire to slow down concerned mobility in particular. Many were those who wanted to spend less time traveling for work and to live more "local" daily lives. Work-related trips were notably mentioned in connection with the desire to slow down:

- 48% expressed the desire to work locally, either at home (30%) or in their neighborhood (18%);
- 13% wished they could work wherever and whenever they wanted.

Considered conjointly, these results suggest a significant gap between the injunction to practice reversible mobility as promoted by European policies and the aspirations of most of Europe's population.

Work-Related High Mobility

After painting this broad picture, we will now focus on highly mobile commuters, whose lifestyles are particularly affected by the intensity of mobile lifestyles.

In the scientific literature, the term "work-related high mobility" is used to describe extreme forms of work-related travel, in other words "mobility to work" (e.g., long-distance or long-term commuting); "mobility in/at work," like frequent business trips; or even "mobility because of work," which relates to living away from the family home for work-related reasons.

Why do we call this "high mobility"? The definitions of mobility and motility that we set out in Chapter 2 help us to better explain this concept: this type of commuting uses the speed potential of transport and telecommunication systems to fend off geographical friction and reconcile what was once spatially irreconcilable. Considered as such, high mobility is distinguished by its reversible nature. "High" therefore refers to the frequency and scope of long-distance travel.

The reversible nature of such mobility characterizes and distinguishes the various forms of high mobility. Rapid transport and telecommunications systems now allow people to live and work in geographically distant places. Reversible mobility is a fundamentally new phenomenon. While history suggests that our ancestors were much more mobile than we often imagine (seasonal migrations were common for work, as was travel), these trips were not reversible and implied a total lack of communication with relatives, often over long periods (e.g., seasonal timeframes).

Job Mobilities and Family Lives Survey: Six Research Findings

We will now empirically address work-related high mobilities based on data from the European "Job Mobilities and Family Lives" research study (hereinafter abbreviated as JobMob) carried out in 2007 and 2011 in Germany, Spain, France and Switzerland (Schneider & Collet, 2010; Schneider & Meil Landwerlin, 2008; Viry & Kaufmann, 2015). In this panel survey, three types of phenomena were considered high mobility:

- "Long-distance commuting," which is defined as spending more than two hours a day commuting in addition to actual working hours.
- "Overnighting," which refers to sleeping away from home for work. The survey only included individuals who spent more than 60 nights a year away from home.
- "Long-distance relationships," where people in a stable couple relationship live in separate homes more than an hour apart for professional reasons.

This research began in 2006 as part of the 6th European Union research framework program. A European survey was then organized to better measure the magnitude of the work-related high mobility phenomenon and how it relates to work and family life. The first part of the study was completed in 2010. The second wave of the survey, which questioned those already interviewed in 2007, was relaunched in 2011.

The survey targeted a representative sample of the working population aged 25 to 54. For the first wave in 2007, 7,220 people in six countries (Germany, Belgium, Spain, France, Poland and Switzerland) were surveyed. For the second wave in four of the six countries (Germany, Spain, France and Switzerland) in 2011 (2012),

1,985 people were surveyed. We will now briefly present several important results that emerged from the analysis of high mobility practices.

The first survey concerned the quantitative scope of these practices. As a result, 15% of the working population in Europe were considered to be "highly mobile" at the time of the survey. Moreover, the survey data highlighted the fact that 50% of the working population had experienced a period of "high mobility" at some point in their working life (see Figure 4.1).

The second key finding concerns the inequalities resulting from and reinforced by high mobility. Our analyses of the JobMob research suggest that high mobility practices reinforce inequalities linked to gender and household composition.

In the 2011 survey, 13% of men were considered long-distance commuters compared to just 7% of women. We found the same disparity among overnighters, where 6% of men were concerned versus only 2% of women.

Regarding family structure, single-parent families differed from other family types, with more than 15% of these individuals either long-distance commuting or overnighting, compared to only 8% of people living with a partner and one or more children. The need for steady income adds to scheduling and organizational constraints, especially when it comes to raising children, which is why these individuals often choose high mobility as a "solution." The research also highlights the lack of stability with regard to high mobility for these individuals, who tended to stop and start high mobility practices more often than others.

Longitudinal data from the JobMob study shows that the strain that high mobility puts on family life often led women to abandon their careers once they had had a child and moreover, indicated a higher divorce rate among couples wherein one of the partners was highly mobile.

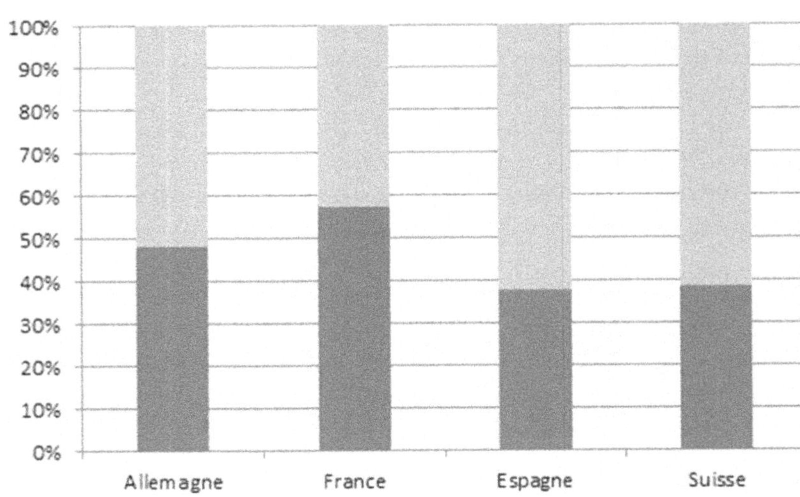

FIGURE 4.1 Percentage of adults aged 30 to 59 who had had a period of high mobility of more than six months in their lives

For women, motherhood effectively marked the end of high mobility, whereas fatherhood changed nothing from this standpoint for men. Among men, 49% who were mobile in 2007 were still mobile in 2011 if they had not had a child, compared to 41% for those who had had one. Among women, 44% remained mobile if they had not had a child between the two waves of the survey, versus only 17% for those who had. More remarkably, none remained highly mobile if the child was their first.

Further statistical analyses also point to a weakening of the marital bond due to high mobility practices that was more prevalent among women without children and men with child(ren).

One thing, however, was true in all cases: high mobility delayed the founding of a family (at least for the first child) for women and men alike. However, gender differences emerged in this area and revealed that high mobility with several children was more compatible with men's careers than women's. Women with highly mobile partners tended to seek jobs closer to home or even stop working altogether. As we can see, all forms of high mobility necessitate immobility, be it in terms of family, transportation or the workplace. One thus remarks that having children tends to reinforce traditional gender roles, with women as the guardians of the hearth in the absence of the mobile spouse. (Note that the opposite is not true of women's mobility, although high mobility does tend to encourage a more equal sharing of domestic tasks.)

The third important finding concerns the lack of a link between high mobility and income levels. While high mobility reinforces gender inequalities linked to family structure, the JobMob research showed, on the contrary, that income did not shape the practice of high mobility. In other words, contrary to popular belief, highly mobile individuals come from both wealthy and modest backgrounds. Education level also had little impact on high mobility practices. With regard to age, our analyses revealed that highly mobile people were not necessarily the youngest members of the workforce.

The fourth key observation is that the disposition to work-related mobility within the population is extremely diverse. Four provisions were identified in this area (see Table 4.1):

- Those not open to mobility (25% in 2007, 31% in 2011) represented a particularly homogeneous group. These individuals stated that they were unwilling to commute or move for their work. The likelihood of falling into this category increased with age. Men were less represented than women, as were single people and single-parent families compared to biparental families with child(ren).
- At the other end of the spectrum were those who were open to any and all forms of mobility (10% in 2007, 13% in 2011). This group was comprised of younger people and included more men than women. These individuals tended to be single or in a couple without children. Family life, it would seem, is not coherent with a strong disposition to mobility. Finally, it should be noted that this category tended to include directors, managers and freelancers (versus "basic" employees).

TABLE 4.1 Characterization of the typology of dispositions to mobility, logistic regressions (expressed in the form of Odds ratio)

	Not open to work-related mobility		*Open to relocating for work*		*Open to reversible mobility*		*Open to all forms of mobility*	
	2007	*2011*	*2007*	*2011*	*2007*	*2011*	*2007*	*2011*
Sex: Women (ref)								
Men	0.43**	0.41**	1.61**	1.79**	1.04	1.20*	1.99**	2.26**
Age: 29–38 (ref.)								
39–48	1.41**	1.29*	0.79*	0.86	1.32*	1.40**	0.52**	0.57**
49–59	2.00**	1.77**	0.47**	0.50**	1.47**	1.53**	0.55**	0.51**
Education level: low (ref.)								
Medium	1.13	1.14	1.48**	1.45**	0.68**	0.71**	0.83	0.77
High	1.00	0.94	2.38**	2.57**	0.47**	0.50**	0.75	0.77
Income level: middle (ref.)								
Low	1.06	0.86	1.04	1.08	0.92	0.87	1.10	1.12
High	0.75*	0.86	1.06	1.02	1.19	1.02	1.12	1.13
Family: lives with partner & child (ref.)								
Lives alone	0.53**	0.63**	1.14	1.03	0.90	0.98	2.08**	2.36**
Lives with a partner	1.01	0.95	0.87	0.87	0.90	0.85	1.53**	1.52**
Lives with a child without a partner	0.48**	0.69*	2.15**	2.01**	0.93	1.02	0.76	0.85
Hierarchy: basic employee (ref.)								
Director/manager	0.86	-	1.49*	-	0.60*	-	1.72*	-
Middle-level position	1.04	-	1.10	-	0.86	-	1.13	-
Freelancer	0.96	-	1.21	-	0.67*	-	1.72*	-
Significance of model	.000	.000	.000	.000	.000	.000	.000	.000
N	2660	3236	2660	3236	2660	3236	2660	3236

* $p < .05$; ** $p < .01$

Source: JobMob II, LaSUR treatment, "countries equally weighted"

- Those open to reversible mobility (32% in 2007, 31% in 2011) were defined by their attachment to their home. As such, they generally rejected the idea of moving to another region or abroad. On the other hand, long-distance commuting or even weekly commuting was an option for them. Such strong ties were mainly observed in older populations with lower levels of training. These individuals tended to be "basic" employees (versus managers or freelancers).
- The final category included those who were willing to move (33% in 2007, 25% in 2011) – though sometimes under specific conditions – but for whom the idea of reversible mobility (daily or weekly) was unappealing.

Respondents' willingness to be mobile grew between 2007 and 2011, which suggests the existence of a growing injunction to mobility in the work world. This is the fifth main finding from the JobMob research data.

A correspondence analysis was carried out to account for the main trends within the four types of mobility positions and to better visualize the changes in people's willingness between 2007 and 2011. The first two axes of the factorial plan account for 87% of the total variance:

- The first axis indicates strong or weak openness to mobility practices. Respondents opposed to mobility were situated at the left, while those open to all forms of mobility were on the right.
- The second axis represents strong or weak openness to reversible mobility practices. At the bottom of this second axis were those willing to partake in reversible mobility. Conversely, those willing to relocate were situated at the top of the axis.

The types of mobility identified between 2007 and 2011 underline the fact that, while changes could be observed for many of the respondents, the former were often partial and concerned their disposition either to reversible mobility or to relocation, but rarely to both. The vast majority, however, reflect increased willingness to be mobile. As such, growing openness to mobility – both reversible and non-reversible forms, such as relocation to another region or abroad – were observed.

The sixth and final key finding that emerged from our analyses of the JobMob panel database was that people who practice highly mobile are not necessarily those most open to doing so.

To study this point, we analyzed the explanatory factors for high mobility for the entire sample as well as for women and men separately in order to also highlight gender differences. Three logistic regression models were thus produced. Model A included respondents' main socio-economic characteristics; model B included their hierarchical position; and model C added a typology of openness to mobility (Table 4.2).

TABLE 4.2 Logistic regressions of high mobility in 2011 (expressed as odd ratios)

	All			*Women*			*Men*		
	A	*B*	*C*	*A*	*B*	*C*	*A*	*B*	*C*
Women	.48**	.51**	.52**						
Age: 29–38 (ref.)									
39–48	1.27	1.28	1.32	.86	.91	1.10	1.57	1.64	1.59
49–59	.98	1.11	1.10	.63	.62	.67	1.21	1.45	1.41
Education level: low (ref.)									
Medium	1.05	1.03	1.01	1.23	1.20	1.13	.90	.91	.91
High	1.09	1.05	1.15	1.36	1.20	1.34	.90	.87	.96
Income level: low (ref.)									
Medium	1.39	1.35	1.40	1.13	1.15	1.05	1.48	1.41	1.44
High	1.48	1.52	1.41	1.08	1.18	.99	1.72	1.70	1.58
Household: in couple with child (ref.)									
Lives alone	2.21**	2.33**	2.24**	3.31**	3.82**	3.15**	1.86*	1.92**	1.99**
Lives with a partner	1.16	1.18	1.31	1.75	2.05	1.97	.99	.97	1.17
Lives without partner w/ child	4.83**	5.17**	5.25**	4.68**	5.41**	4.77**	9.84**	9.45**	10.12**
Hierarchy: low-level position (ref.)									
Director/manager		.66	.70		1.54	1.92		.41	.47
Mid-level position		1.12	1.09		2.05*	2.15*		.77	.74
Freelancer		.85	.88		2.02	1.94		.53	.57
Openness to mobility: not open (ref.)									
Open to relocating			1.57			.76			2.33*
Open to reversible mobility			3.25**			1.80			4.84**
Open to all forms of mobility			2.56**			2.62*			2.90*
Constant	.08**	.08**	.04**	.04**	.04**	.03**	.07**	.09**	.03**
-2 log-likelihood model	1045.12	936.56	904.84	411.47	341.25	328.07	623.30	584.53	556.42
χ^2	45.74	41.04	69.28	21.37	26.32	32.68	21.76	23.59	48.38
Degree of freedom	10	13	16	9	12	15	9	12	15
Significance of the model	.000	.000	.000	.011	.010	.005	.010	.023	.000
Pseudo R^2 (Nagelkerke)	.06	.06	.10	.06	.09	.12	.05	.06	.11
N	1714	1358	1337	999	746	733	715	612	604

* $p < .05$; ** $p < .01$; weighted data

Source: JobMob II, LaSUR analyses

The results of the analysis show that women were significantly less mobile than men in 2011, even among the working population. Strikingly, neither the age nor the education level nor the income level of male and female respondents significantly influenced their high mobility practices. Nevertheless, higher-income respondents tended to be more mobile than those with lower incomes, but this effect was not significant at only 5%. It was above all household composition that influenced high mobility. People living alone and single parents were more likely to be highly mobile than those with a partner and children. This was the case for both men and women. Single people were effectively less bound by domestic obligations than those in couples. As such, regular absences from home for work-related reasons raised fewer issues. Individuals in long-distance relationships by definition also fell into this category. Single working parents (and single mothers in particular) had little choice but to long-distance commute due to their unique role as head of household. Respondents' hierarchical position did not have a significant effect on the probability of them being highly mobile (with the exception of women managers, who were more likely to be mobile than women without hierarchical responsibilities).

Finally, individuals' disposition to mobility strongly explains mobility practices, especially among men. Among these individuals, those with a disposition to reversible mobility, those open to all forms of mobility and those willing to relocate were more highly mobile than those unopen to any form of mobility. This effect was particularly strong among sedentary men. Among women, only those open to all forms of mobility were more mobile. It thus appeared that mobile men were more willing to travel than their female counterparts, and that non-mobile men were more willing to be mobile than non-mobile women. However, the effect of the willingness to be mobile did not impact the other effects. In other words, the greater mobility of men, of people living alone and of single parents was not due these groups' greater willingness to be mobile.

Yet, looking more closely, one notes considerable differences in the relationship between people's disposition to mobility and high mobility practices between the different countries studied. The relationships between dispositions and high mobility diverged in the four countries that partook in both waves of the survey (2007 and 2011), with Spain standing out.

Germany (in the first wave) and Spain (in the second wave) stood out for their respondents' strong willingness to long-distance commute. The increase in this indicator between the two survey waves in Spain was striking. In this category, men, the youngest age group, the most educated, childless individuals, and people in supervisory positions were the most willing to long-distance commute to further their careers. We also found that having a job and individuals' income level were not closely associated with a disposition to high mobility in 2007 but became more so in 2011. In Spain, for instance, low-income and unemployed individuals developed a strong willingness to long-distance commute in the second wave.

Here we noted a particularly strong two-fold change in Spanish respondents' behavior, who were at once less mobile and yet more willing to be so in 2011 than in 2007. It would seem that for them (or many of them), being open to mobility meant adapting their lifestyle criteria to a particularly difficult labor market. Effectively, Spain underwent a major economic crisis between the two waves of the survey, which resulted in a significant rise in unemployment.

Between 2007 and 2011, Spanish respondents became increasingly open to relocating to another region of their country (27% compared with 13% of Germans, 6% of French and 17% of Swiss), relocating abroad (24% versus 8%, 12% and 12% respectively), long-distance commuting (40% versus 23%, 15% and 21% respectively), weekly commuting (37% compared with 11%, 17% and 8% respectively) and even regular business travel (33% compared with 18%, 29% and 18% respectively) than respondents from the other three countries. Conversely, Spanish respondents were likely to be among those with the fewest skills for dealing with long-distance mobility, although they were considering it.

The results for Spain revealed an openness to imposed mobility, or in other words an injunction to high mobility. While we noted a strong capacity for adaptation and certain flexibility on the part of the Spanish as regards the employment situation in the 2011 survey, these conditions were nonetheless imposed. As such, individuals find themselves having to juggle career advancement and their personal lives. While high mobility is one way of reconciling the two, difficulty finding a job limits aspirations relative to family life.

Conclusion

This chapter explored a number of trends in the development of mobilities in European lifestyles, first using recent surveys carried out by the Mobile Lives Forum and then by focusing on people who travel fast, far and frequently for work each day.

These investigations demonstrate the fact that lifestyles are becoming increasingly fast paced, especially as regards work, and that freedom of movement has gradually become an injunction to mobility. Highly mobile individuals are emblematic of this phenomenon. Their lifestyles demand particularly intensive forms of mobility. One might think that this incessant movement is a source of fulfillment and positive self-transformation. Yet, the JobMob panel survey data suggests the opposite; on the contrary, high mobility exacerbates gender inequalities, weakens couple relationships and is seemingly an inherent constraint in a job market characterized by a growing demand for temporal and spatial flexibility. Time is optimized, and free time is gobbled up – a far cry from the ideal of the mobile senior executive whose life is punctuated by rewarding business trips.

Free movement in Europe thus appears in the harsh light of an injunction to mobility that is imposed on managers, employees and workers alike, on those willing to be mobile as well as on those who are not.

Note

1. This is the case with halved workdays, which generate four home-work trips instead of two, as with, for instance, office cleaning staff who come in early in the morning and again late at night.

References

Forum Vies Mobiles. (2016). *Aspirations liées à la mobilité et aux modes de vie – Enquête internationale, édition 2015*. Paris: Forum Vies Mobiles & l'OBSOCO.

Forum Vies Mobiles. (2020). *Enquête nationale mobilité et modes de vie, édition 2019*. Paris: Forum Vies Mobiles & l'OBSOCO.

Kaufmann, V., Ravalet, E., & Drevon, G. (2020). *Mesurer la motilité par un indice opérationnel*. Lausanne: EPFL.

Le Breton, É. (2005). *Bouger pour s'en sortir: Mobilité quotidienne et intégration sociale*. Paris: Armand Colin.

Le Marchand, A. (2011). *Enclaves nomades: Habitat et travail mobiles*. Bellecombe-en-Bauges: Éditions du Croquant.

Mincke, C., & Montulet, B. (2019). *La société sans répit: La mobilité comme injonction*. Paris: Editions de la Sorbonne.

Ravalet, E., Vincent-Geslin, S., Kaufmann, V., & Leveugle, J. (2014). *Slices of (mobile) life: A sociological study and manifesto on work-related high mobility*. Paris: Loco & Forum Vies Mobiles.

Ravalet, E., Vincent-Geslin, S., Kaufmann, V., Viry, G., & Dubois, Y. (2015). *Grandes mobilités liées au travail: Perspective européenne*. Paris: Economica.

Schneider, N. F., & Collet, B. (Eds.). (2010). *Mobile living across Europe II: Causes and consequences of job-related spatial mobility in cross-national comparison*. Opladen: Barbara Budrich Publishers.

Schneider, N. F., & Meil Landwerlin, G. (Eds.). (2008). *Mobile living across Europe I: Relevance and diversity of job-related spatial mobility in six European countries*. Opladen: Barbar Budrich Publishers.

Sergot, B., Chabault, D., & Loubaresse, É. (2012). Mobilités spatiales et dynamiques organisationnelles. *Revue Francaise De Gestion, N° 226*, 77–90.

Viry, G., & Kaufmann, V. (Eds.). (2015). *High mobility in Europe: Work and personal life*. Houndmills, Basingstoke Hampshire: Palgrave Macmillan.

5

TOWARDS NEW PERSPECTIVES OF COHESION FOR CROSS-BORDER AREAS

Introduction

The European question and cooperation among Member States more specifically are often on the margins of major electoral campaigns, political programs and debates between candidates, even at the local level in cross-border urban regions. European elections are arguably the least publicized ballot and those with the lowest turnout, and the abstention rate continues to grow throughout the EU. In addition, the press's focus on European failures in recent years (e.g., the inability to take a common stance in international crises, the lack of solidarity among member countries as regards hosting refugees during successive crises in the Middle East and more recently the flagrant lack of health coordination in managing the COVID-19 pandemic) have done little to remedy the situation.

Budget austerity and negative press have created a sense of mistrust and dissension vis-à-vis Europe and its institutions. These feelings have led to a resurgence of populist rhetoric and sovereigntist/independentist trends in many Member countries such as the United Kingdom, whose exit from the EU was unprecedented. For many European citizens, Europe and its institutions seem distant, as they ultimately have little impact on everyday life. Moreover, in this era of dissension vis-à-vis the European Agenda, territories are confronted by its various integration projects in an unequal way. This inequality is most pronounced in France, one of the founding members of the EU. With its centralized model, France tends to abandon its border regions in favor of larger cities. The former's development is left to the charge of European collaboration and integration programs. Residents of such areas are therefore directly confronted with European integration and cooperation policies. In this way, cross-border urban regions bear witness to the successes and failures of the European project whose driving forces must be understood both spatially and socially. This means having an overarching perspective on the plurality of heritages,

DOI: 10.4324/9780429325014-5

configurations and relationships of and between urban cross-border regions. This chapter also aims to explore new avenues for considering cross-border relations, particularly based on new analytical methods for studying cross-border spaces. For our exploration, we will place cross-border urban regions within the political apparatus of the EU.

The European Agenda and Difficulties in Linking Various Levels of Cooperation

European treaties (the Treaty of Rome, Treaty of Maastricht, etc.) are most often forged from a perspective of interstate cooperation and aim to reconcile a group of nation states. This involves reflection at the interstate level (e.g., Southern Common Market (MERCOSUR) and United States-Mexico-Canada Agreement (USMCA)) and favors international exchanges with regard to the mobility of goods, people and services. However, it overlooks the subnational and subregional scales. Although free trade agreements have greatly facilitated cooperation between European states – especially economically – they tend to face difficulties in cross-border regions. Effectively, and although certain cross-border areas such as the Greater Luxembourg Region, Greater Geneva and the Basel cross-border area must address numerous economic and strategic issues that are key for the future of European integration, cooperation strategies struggle to create cross-border integrated development projects in all areas of land use planning (transport, city planning, waste management).

Roughly 30 years later and in the wake of the European construction, social scientists have carefully observed the different scales of European cooperation. Economists have largely sought to measure the economic impact of the single market and greatly assisted in analyzing the barrier effects of borders on trade flows and business transactions in cross-border regions. The analysis of border differentials has also been widely explored in economics literature. Geography and spatial analysis have been instrumental in analyzing the configurations of urban spaces and cross-border cities. Sociology, anthropology and language sciences have also delved into the question of cross-border regions to better grasp cross-border relations by considering differentials linked to identity, language and national affiliation. Cross-border regions are therefore complex entities wherein the effects of European agreements have repercussions at the local level, affording development opportunities on one hand and tensions on the other. Urban cross-border regions are also characterized by important specificities in terms of their geography, as demonstrated in particular by urban configurations, the cohabitation of languages and cultures and their historical heritage.

Border Heritage as a Barrier

From the perspective of European construction, borders were rapidly seen as barriers to be circumvented. This conception is linked to European heritage, wherein border issues have typically been military or customs related. Beyond historical considerations, which treated borders as barriers, abundant literature has highlighted the effects of discontinuity, particularly spatial and economic. Discontinuity is characterized by differentiation in territorial organization on either side of the border (Hamez et al., 2011). From an epistemological standpoint, they are part and parcel of the study of territorial discontinuity (i.e., ruptures along the boundaries of territories) (Grasland, 1997; Taillefer, 1970). From a spatial analysis perspective, it is an exception observed in a global context of spatial autocorrelation (Grasland, 1997).

In other words, these discontinuities can be observed in a break between two territorial entities with homogeneous characteristics based on a synthetic indicator (population, urbanization). If the territorial discontinuity observed through the statistical break coincides with the presence of a border, one can speak of border discontinuity. Work on border discontinuity in the Schengen area falls in the wake of European construction.

The main goal is to measure the regional effects of the opening of borders on socio-economic interactions and territorial cohesion. French geographer Claude Grasland has greatly contributed to the understanding of discontinuities and inequalities in Europe, and has highlighted important internal discontinuities within states and between European regions (Grasland, 1997). This work was subsequently used through the concept of territorial cohesion between European regions (Grasland & Hamez, 2005). Based on the GDP, unemployment rate and population's age in different European regions, the authors identify three types of territorial discontinuities that may hamper territorial cohesion. The first (type A) corresponds to important differentials in the wealth and age of the population (e.g., the first region is economically comfortable and has a young population while the second is poorer and has an older population). The second (type B) is characteristic of the functional differentiation between metropolitan regions with centralized financial and economic power (e.g., Ile de France) and neighboring regions (Picardy). The third (type C) concerns a significant wealth differential between a region with considerable interaction between cross-border workers and other regions (e.g., Wallonia, Lorraine, Rhineland-Palatinate), and those marked by disadvantages (e.g., Saar).

These three types of discontinuities, which are not necessarily modeled on state borders, also correspond to interregional discontinuities at the intra-national level. Barriers, a concept related to discontinuities, also helps in understanding the effects of borders on the surrounding territories. Borders as geographical limits can create a barrier effect. This phenomenon is generally highlighted by weaker flows between the regions surrounding the border versus interactions with neighboring regions in the same country. Weaker flows between regions separated by a border would thus indicate a barrier effect (Hamez et al., 2011). Such effects can be generated by spatial (topography or distance), economic (cost) or regulatory (taxation, jurisdiction) factors. Rietveld (2012) distinguishes five types of border barriers from an economic standpoint. The first is consumer preference for products from their country of residence (Hofstede, 1984). The second is taxes on imported products, which can limit the flow of goods from abroad (Anderson & van Wincoop, 2004). The third is institutional and legal labor market frameworks on either side of the border, which may prohibit the hiring of foreigners or limit their numbers (Velde, 2004). The fourth is a lack of information due to obstacles to its circulation, combined with national preference (Cappellin, Batey, & Cappelin, 1993). The inexistence or high cost of cross-border transport infrastructure is the fifth barrier (Vickerman, 1994). This last point reinforces the postulate of border-related barriers hampering the daily mobility of cross-border workers in terms of flows (Nijkamp, Rietveld, & Salomon, 1990) as a modal shift (Schiebel, Omrani, & Gerber, 2015).

The lack of information on transport services for border populations also limits daily or occasional mobility. The infrastructural effects of borders are an integral part of the living environments of border residents. These effects, which exist at the macro level, are particularly palpable in the housing market and in transport networks, thereby confirming border effects on the daily lives of their populations. While this literature presents borders as obstacles, actual mobility practices seem to contradict this position; border workers cross the border each day to get to their workplaces. The border is an attractive element just begging to be crossed (border transcending). And yet, it is present in individuals' imaginaries and can even act as a mental barrier (Gerber, 2012). National borders can effectively be considered a political and social construct (Newman, 2003) that is shared and recognized by social groups and is anchored in individuals' social representations, thus implying social heteronomy.

The source of this distinction stems directly from the politico-spatial configuration, which is reflected at the level of social groups through socio-cultural discontinuities (language, practices, codes and customs). Effects at the individual level occur in two ways: first, through the distinction between places on either side of the border according to individuals' nationality and place of residence (this observation is valid for cross-border urban regions as well as at the international, interregional, urban and local levels) and through the symbolic dimension of the border as an intangible object (van Houtum, 2005) (which therefore falls within the realm of the imaginary by associating places with the iconography of which they are the object) (Hamez, 2004). In terms of the separation effect between populations, barriers exist in the form of cultural, socio-cultural and linguistic disparities. Their efficiency has been amply studied (Nijkamp et al., 1990). Thus, for instance, Walloons tend to stay in the French-speaking part of Belgium (Poulain & Foulon, 1998). Although this example concerns linguistic borders within sovereign countries, it attests to the memory of past borders following state unification, of which language distinction is an emblematic example (Dujardin, 2001). Barrier effects linked to language are a widespread phenomenon and cannot be reduced to these examples. As the aforementioned literature suggests, border regions are durably marked by key territorial, infrastructural, economic, social and linguistic discontinuities. Reducing these discontinuities has always been a central issue for

European integration policies since the EU's birth. However, these policies also generate rebound effects, which lead to political forms of nationalist convictions.

The Paradoxical Effects of Debordering and Rebordering

The concept of cross-border integration has strongly marked European public policies over the past 30 years. These policies have established integration observatories like the ESPON program, which aims to measure the dynamics of European cooperation and territorial cohesion, and cooperation mechanisms such as the INTERREG programs, which promotes cross-border cooperation, and European Grouping of Territorial Cooperation, which overcomes the difficulties at the territorial level. These measures focus mainly on economic development, land use planning and environmental conservation and, on the whole, have been largely (Bavoux & Chapelon, 2014) supported by the spatial planning sciences (namely geography and political science). It is from the issue of integration and, by extension, that of cohesion that the field of border studies has developed and flourished in the past 30 years (Newman, 2006). Cross-border integration, a major component of border studies, is based on three key approaches (van Houtum, 2000).

The first, which is functional, involves measuring interactions namely through the analysis of trade flows between territories on the other side of the border. It also incorporates morphological approaches to the border, which mainly concern cross-border urban configurations (Bavoux & Chapelon, 2014). The second approach focuses more on the analysis of European public policies and the analysis of cooperation arrangements. This approach – by actors or institutions – is based mainly on the socio-political logic that underlies the desire to cooperate on one hand and obstacles to cross-border cooperation on the other. The individual approach to integration has to do with the symbols and representations associated with territories and populations situated on either side of the border. It also concerns the intricacy and compatibility of affiliations, identities and forms of attachment from a transnational perspective. By highlighting the drivers of integration or, conversely, the obstacles that limit it, these different approaches have helped in shedding light on the complex processes of *debordering* and *rebordering*. Debordering can be described as the free movement of goods and people, primarily through the phenomenon of cross-border work (Drevon, 2016; Mathä & Wintr, 2009). Border work, which is part of the flow-based integration approach, is effectively an excellent indicator of functional cross-border integration arrangements. The urban regions of Luxembourg, Geneva and Basel are therefore particularly well integrated cross-border areas from a functional standpoint. The latter two also have a particularly well-integrated urban framework and, from a spatio-functional perspective, are emblematic of integrated cross-border territorial configurations. However, and as Critical Geography in particular suggests, functional integration is not necessarily a guarantee of social cohesion between the populations on either side of the border.

Thus, individual and institutional approaches to integration show several forms of border rebordering in Europe. Tension and populist reactions are emerging in cross-border urban regions in response to the opening of borders and the liberalization of trade. This has repercussions at the local level. The dissension is mainly rooted in the sharing of resources, such as the labor market, labor pool, real estate market and even cultural offerings and leisure activities. Differentials in salary levels and land or real estate prices, for example, create dissension between populations and organizations on both sides of the border. Dissension also arises as a result of the confrontation between national ownership of resources and their cross-border use. The crystallizing of these tensions around border issues renders cross-border relations more difficult, especially as regards the labor market, the cornerstone of social conflicts. Border work is therefore one of the emblematic indicators of tensions that affect cross-border cities, particularly in Switzerland. Cross-border commuters are often seen as opportunistic and as having excursionist, economically oriented cross-border mobility. Some proponents of regulating the number of cross-border commuters believe that employing foreign cross-border workers leads to lower wages and increased unemployment due to greater competition with the local workforce.

This argument serves as a basis for political dissension that targets border workers, and both fuels and justifies anti-border positions in several countries, including Switzerland. As a corollary, cross-border workers are also strongly criticized in their country of residence. Their buying power versus that of other residents effectively drives real estate prices up. This cross-border gentrification, which, for now, has been little explored in the scientific research, pushes non-cross-border workers to move away to the benefit of border workers. This process of socio-spatial segregation (for instance, on the border areas of Luxembourg and the Canton of Geneva) fuels dissension between workers and border residents. The psychosocial dimension of the relationship between the territory and populations on the other side of the border is also a central element (e.g., the choice of locations concerning business activities). In this context, the social relations established between the inhabitants of urban cross-border regions vary from openness (debordering) to reassertion of the border (rebordering) (Balogh, 2013).

The rebordering phenomenon is particularly salient in cross-border urban regions where the number of cross-border workers is high. In Switzerland, for instance, this has materialized in the form of recurring debates on work permit quotas and the emergence of anti-border political movements such as the MCG (Geneva Citizens' Movement), which campaigns in defense of Geneva residents with national and cantonal labor market preference. Thus, rebound effects notably appear at the level of urban cross-border regions, which are heavily marked by functional integration, the case of Geneva being emblematic with the rise of populist and protectionist movements. More notably, this finding supports critical geography theses by confirming that functional integration is not necessarily a guarantee of social cohesion. Paradoxically, functional integration improves flows of exchanges and interactions, but also causes friction at the local level. For example, the opening of borders intensifies competition for jobs, leads to the flight of skilled labor to the country with the highest salary and promotes price convergence in the land and real estate markets, which impacts transport networks. All of these rebound effects undermine social and territorial cohesion by granting comparative advantages associated with the presence of a national border to certain social classes or privileged actors. Thus does the debordering/rebordering pair generate considerable paradoxical effects that fuel dissension in cross-border regions. One possible explanation lies in European public policies' inability to seize upon the plurality of cross-border regions in terms of geography, language and culture.

The Many Forms of Borders and Border Cities

The forms and functions of national borders have been the subject of a host of analogies under the umbrella of geography. Among these, the sewn border/cut border duo has long prevailed. This analogy points to the ambivalent, attraction/repulsion qualities of borders. The border has also been called a synapse, given cross-border networks' ability to connect territories and populations on either side of the border. Jean-Jacques Bavoux and Laurent Chapelon's dictionary of spatial analysis (Bavoux & Chapelon, 2014) proposes no less than 30 morpho-functional functions of borders (see Figure 5.1). These functions are grouped into five categories. The first is the border as a vague subset, which refers, for example, to disputed areas and no man's lands. The second is the border as a barrier to trade, and thus concerning natural and political ruptures and discontinuities. Third, the border generates economic differentials in terms of more attractive wages, real estate and/or

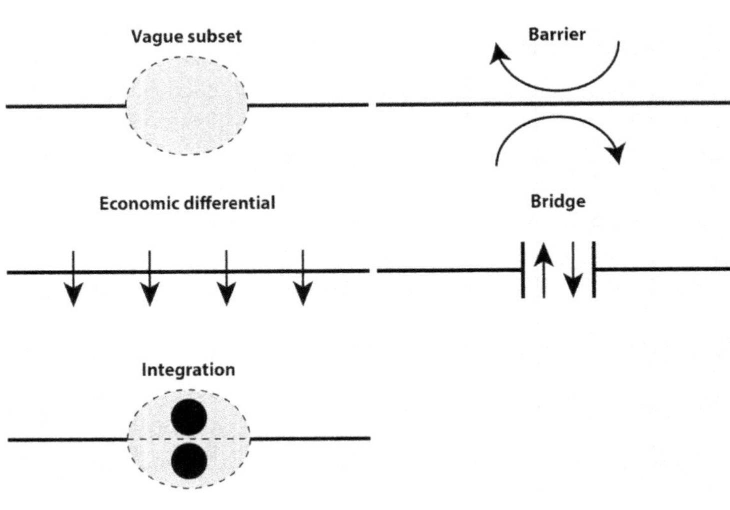

FIGURE 5.1 The 5 morpho-functional forms of the border according to (Bavoux & Chapelon, 2014)

land prices on one side of the border than the other. Fourth, the border acts as an opening, a bridge between two territories and/or the erasure of borders' historical functions. Finally, the border as an attractive area that reflects a unique example of integration. Although theoretical, these morpho-functional categories highlight the plurality of forms and functions of borders and dynamics at work in cross-border areas. Several morpho-functional forms can coexist within a single cross-border urban region. Their overlapping in such areas shows the complexity of the relationship between transborder areas.

The works of Christophe Sohn and Nora Stambolic are an enlightening contribution to the topic of forms of urban cross-border regions. The authors identify four main categories based on a functional analysis of cross-border relations (Sohn & Stambolic, 2015). The first category corresponds to urban cross-border regions, the second to urban border regions, the third to border regions under a metropolitan influence and the fourth to border regions with urban potential. According to the authors, the first type concerns cases where the urban center is situated in the immediate vicinity of the border (Types 1 and 2, Figure 5.1). This is the case of Geneva, Lille, Basel and Strasbourg, for instance, which fall into a monocentric metropolitan category. Other cases, which follow the polycentric model, seem to be unique to northern countries (e.g., Copenhagen-Malmö and Vienna-Bratislava). This first category is marked by intense flows of cross-border workers and numerous cooperation and integration mechanisms in these regions.

The second category concerns metropolitan border regions. In this case, the metropolitan center is located at some distance from the border; its zone of influence is limited to the surrounding peri-urban area and cross-border relations are limited. Emblematic cities in this second category include Milan, Brussels, Zurich and Budapest. The third category concerns border regions under the double influence of a metropolitan area on one side and a national border on the other. According to Sohn and Stambolic, Germany, which effectively is comprised of large urban hubs (Berlin, Munich, Stuttgart and Hamburg) situated relatively far from the national border, is emblematic of this form. Therefore, these hubs, which are nevertheless located in border regions, have limited cooperation with neighboring countries. The fourth category is border regions with high urban potential but no metropolitan center of international stature. Generally polycentric, these border regions are marked by old cooperation mechanisms and strong cultural and socio-economic interactions. Some examples include the German-Dutch border region and the Bayonne-San Sebastian cross-border area.

These functional categories, which are typical of urban border regions, highlight the variety of configurations possible in cross-border relations. They also show certain regional specificities and divisions, for instance between Western and Eastern Europe and between North and South. The eastern border of France is strongly marked by cross-border metropolitan regions. In fact, the Lille-Luxembourg-Strasbourg-Basel-Geneva backbone is a testament to a level of functional integration that is unique in Europe and revolves around major metropolitan and political centers. This backbone is also marked by intense cross-border cooperation

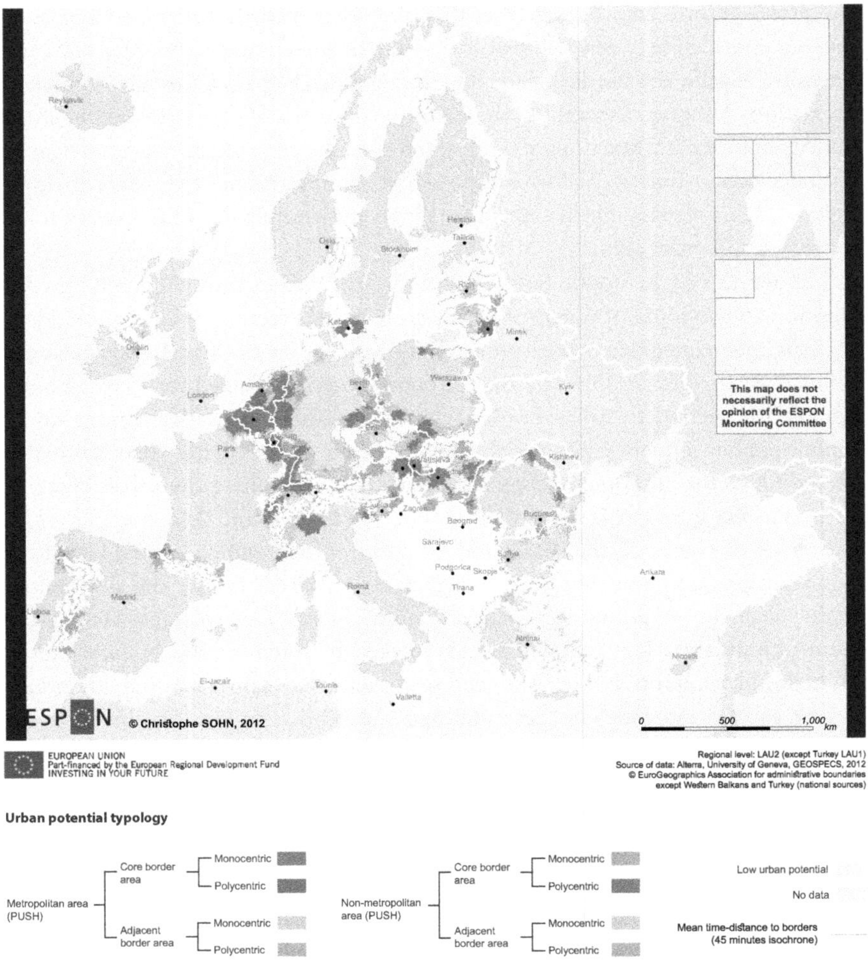

FIGURE 5.2 Urban potential of functional border regions in Europe (Sohn & Stambolic, 2015)

measures. With the exception of Vienna and Bratislava, functional border configurations in Eastern Europe are based on networks of small towns. The dynamics of cross-border interactions are relatively weak insofar as these areas have been facing major industrial and demographic decline for several years now. Southern European borders, which are for the most part sparsely urbanized, are also marked by cross-border interactions with low levels of integration. These differences attest to major rifts within the EU; on one hand, while the historically founding countries of the EU benefit from dynamic border and cross-border urban regions where wealth and capital abound, Eastern and Southern European countries must deal with border regions where the stakes, especially economic ones, are much lower.

Social Trust: Beyond Functional Integration

Although Europe enjoys border and cross-border metropolitan layouts that are conducive to key forms of cross-border integration, debates between proponents of functionalist and individual approaches remain lively, especially given the acute tensions in certain cross-border areas such as Greater Geneva. The scientific debate is primarily based on the impact of development policies and cooperation in terms of social cohesion in cross-border regions. Antoine Decoville and Frédéric Durand's recent research is particularly interesting in this regard (Durand & Decoville, 2020). By reconciling the three approaches to cross-border integration (flow, cooperation and individual) in a single indicator, these researchers have shown significant rifts between the different EU regions. Based on a European survey of 40,619 people (Eurobarometer), they measured the number of activities individuals partook in abroad in cross-border regions over the course of a year. To measure resident populations' perception of their neighbors, respondents were asked to assess their level of comfort were a person living on the other side of the border to become their work colleague, hierarchical superior, neighbor or a member of their family. The researchers also measured the intensity of cross-border cooperation based on the number of actors involved in the INTERREG A program in each border region, thus demonstrating local actors' willingness to participate in a cross-border cooperation project.

The segmented results of the study (Figure 5.3) show contrasting situations in European regions. From a functional standpoint, border regions in Germany are particularly well integrated, with regular movement between Germany and bordering countries. In contrast, Eastern and Southern European countries – and Northern ones to a lesser extent – had less interaction. Involvement in cross-border cooperation programs like INTERREG differed less according to a West vs. East and North vs. South logic. This notably reflects a willingness on the part of the various actors to cooperate and develop common projects. The perception of neighboring populations in different border regions was an especially interesting point. On one hand, Northern populations felt perfectly at ease with the idea of welcoming someone from the other side of the border into their business or even their family. This observation was also valid for France and its eastern neighbors. The Swiss and Germans also viewed the integration of people from neighboring countries into their immediate social environment in a relatively positive light. In accordance with previous results, Eastern and certain Southern European countries were less inclined to easily accept the arrival of a newcomer into their daily lives. Strong asymmetry also prevailed at the border between Portugal and Spain. While Spanish residents said they felt rather comfortable with the integration of a Portuguese resident into their immediate social environment, the opposite was not true. In this instance, we observed the same level of mistrust vis-à-vis foreigners as in Eastern European countries. The English Channel was also the scene of strong dissension, as a French person's acceptance of the arrival of an English person in their immediate social environment – and vice versa – was not perceived as comfortable

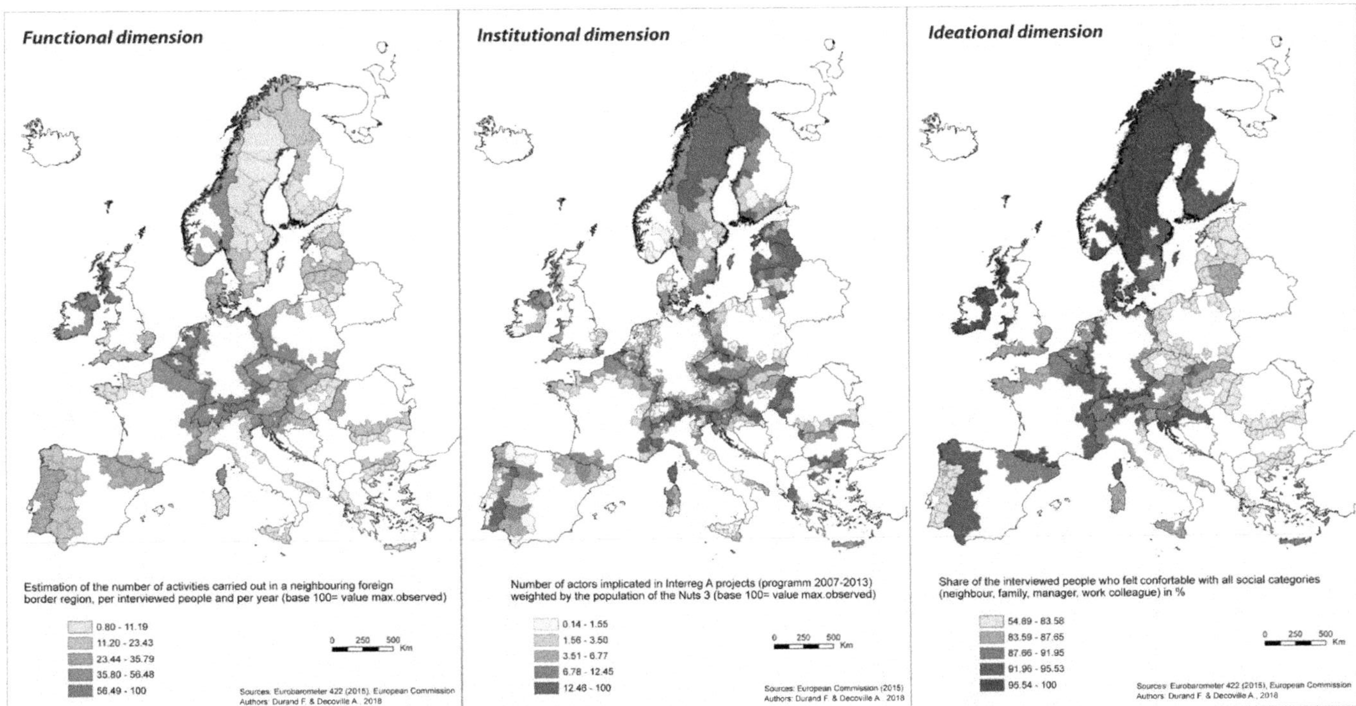

FIGURE 5.3 Multidimensional mapping of the cross-border integration process (Durand & Decoville, 2020)

by either population. It is also important to note the positive reciprocal perceptions of Scottish and Irish populations.

The integration indicator, which combines the three dimensions, is summarized in Figure 5.4. The results confirm the observations mentioned above. On one hand, the integration indicator shows significant cross-border "seams," and on the other, areas of weak integration (functionally, institutionally and socially). Cross-border integration is particularly strong on France's eastern border, as well as on Swiss borders and the majority of German ones. Strong integration was also observed at the Irish border and between the Scandinavian countries. Slovenia also had high levels of integration with its neighboring countries. Observations in Eastern and Southern Europe confirm the aforementioned results. For instance, cross-border integration was weak between Greece and Bulgaria, the Baltic countries, France and England, and to a lesser extent between France and Spain, and between Spain and Portugal.

Daily Experiences of the Border

The integration approach presented above is fairly widespread in the field of border studies. It allows researchers to precisely measure the quality of the relations between European territories and populations on either side of the border. However, other avenues must still be explored in order to supplement spatio-functional integration approaches in particular, which are based on several branches of the social sciences dedicated to understanding professional and exceptional mobility practices (e.g., consumer practices). These approaches have focused on specific populations such as border workers. While the literature on cross-border workers highlights flows and the changes therein as evidence of different degrees of spatio-functional integration (i.e., the first cross-border integration approach), more recent work based mainly on the theoretical and methodological corpus of time geography have attempted to hone the measuring of integration through flows using a disaggregated approach. The analytical tools used in this approach focus on the daily distribution of activities and time spent on either side of the border. From this perspective, time geography and the activities-based approach to mobility more generally seem relevant, as they reveal the breakdown of daily activities in time and space. Time geography effectively takes into account individuals' activities in space and time (Hägerstraand, 1970; Schönfelder & Axhausen, 2010). This approach could therefore be of great use in analyzing cross-border relations, as opposed to analyses of flows of cross-border workers. These analyses, which are still rare in the field of border studies, provide an in-depth understanding of trans-border residents' activity schedules. For example, based on the case of the Greater Luxembourg region, Drevon, Gerber, Klein, and Enaux (2016) (Figure 5.4) identify five behavioral profiles of frontier workers in Luxembourg – commuters, "home-centered," integrated, dispersed and hybrid – depending on the location of the activities undertaken and time spent in the countries of work and residence

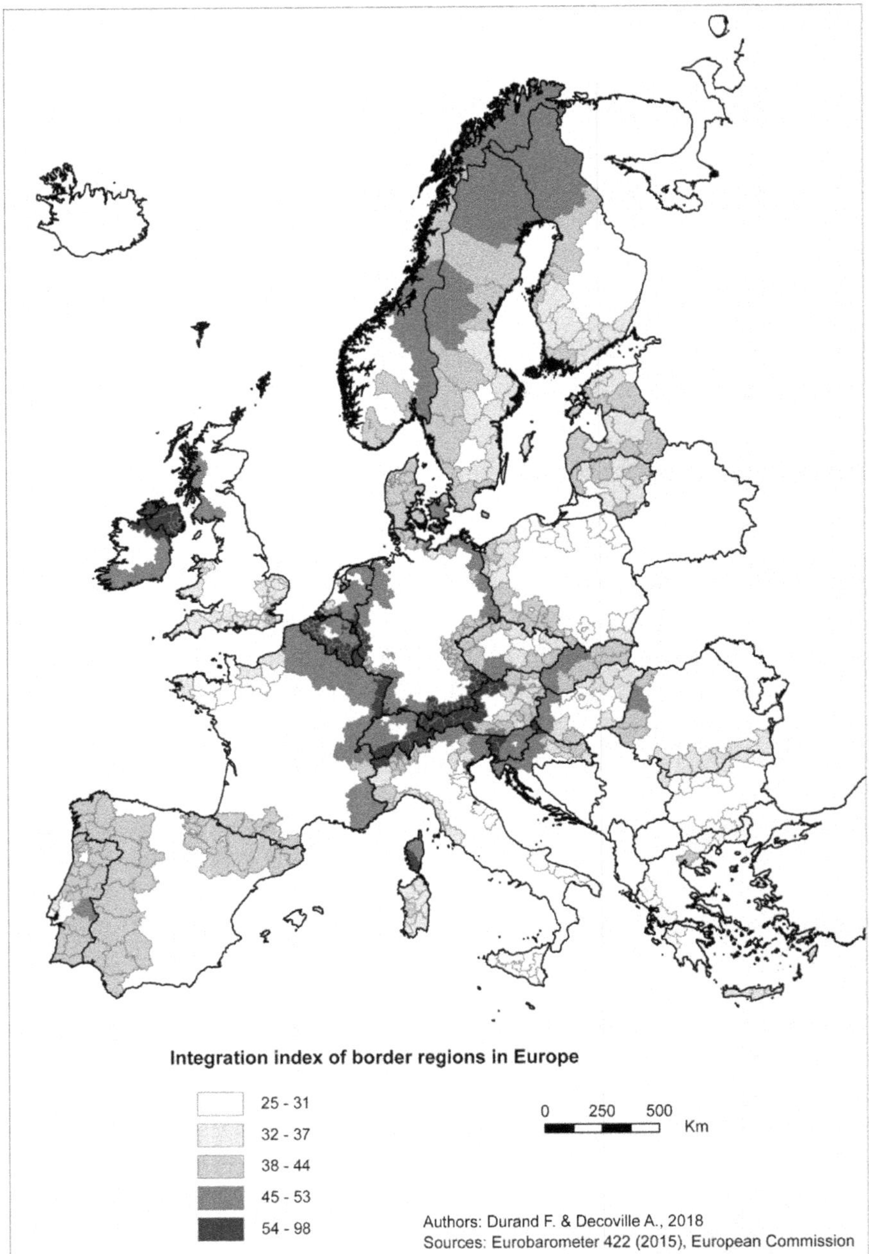

FIGURE 5.4 Integration index of border regions in Europe (Durand & Decoville, 2020)

respectively. This new approach helps highlight the fact that cross-border areas are marked by the coexistence of different ways of inhabiting cross-border regions. By showing the diversity of daily spatio-temporal arrangements in cross-border areas in this way, thinking on the latter tends to echo that of lifestyles, which refers to the "arrangement of daily activities and experiences that give meaning and shape to the lives of a person or group in time and space" (Pattaroni, 2013). The life-style approach sheds light on the social and spatial factors that can potentially limit border crossing and access to resources, such as the labor market, businesses and services. Recent research on Greater Geneva effectively shows that, compared to non-border workers, cross-border workers enjoy a relatively advantageous position that allows them to access all cross-border resources both professionally and residentially. This new perspective for cross-border integration should shed light on different regimes of involvement vis-à-vis the prospect of crossing national borders (e.g., linked to mobility capacities, a sense of national belonging or the arrangement of social networks) (Dubois, 2017, 2019).

Attachment to Place

Beyond daily mobility practices, the analysis of consumer practices is also an important dimension in the study of cross-border relations (Spierings & Velde, 2008; Spierings & Velde, 2013). The authors identify three such types of practices. In this case, the status of cross-border commuters is not determined by their place of work but by their consumption patterns. The first refers to recreational shopping practices, the aim of which is to change the consumption context and concerns consumer subjectivity. The second and third types (purposeful shopping and daily shopping respectively) are characterized by economically oriented objectives, namely a comparative advantage. These three types of consumer practices are driven by different motives. Consumers distinguish places through subjective and symbolic dimensions on one hand and economic ones on the other. The authors consider another interesting dimension based on the concept of "unfamiliarity." Unfamiliarity refers to the unknown dimension of the "other side of the border." Depending on consumer profiles, this dimension can be either attractive or repulsive. Recreational consumer practices, for instance, are a motivational factor for crossing the border (attractive unfamiliarity). However, in the case of economically oriented practices, it can act as a barrier that combines with unattractive consumer costs, comparatively speaking (Spierings & Velde, 2013). The authors introduce the idea of "familiarization," a process by which individuals positively or negatively accustom themselves to the "other side of the border" through consumer practices. Repeated frequentation of places across the border can help forge feelings of attachment or, conversely, rejection based on the individual's judgment. Regular or occasional cross-border mobility therefore plays a role in the building of cross-border identity through individual practices. The consumer practice approach sheds light on the distinction effect between transborder areas and people's image of the "other side" based on individual attraction and repulsion effects.

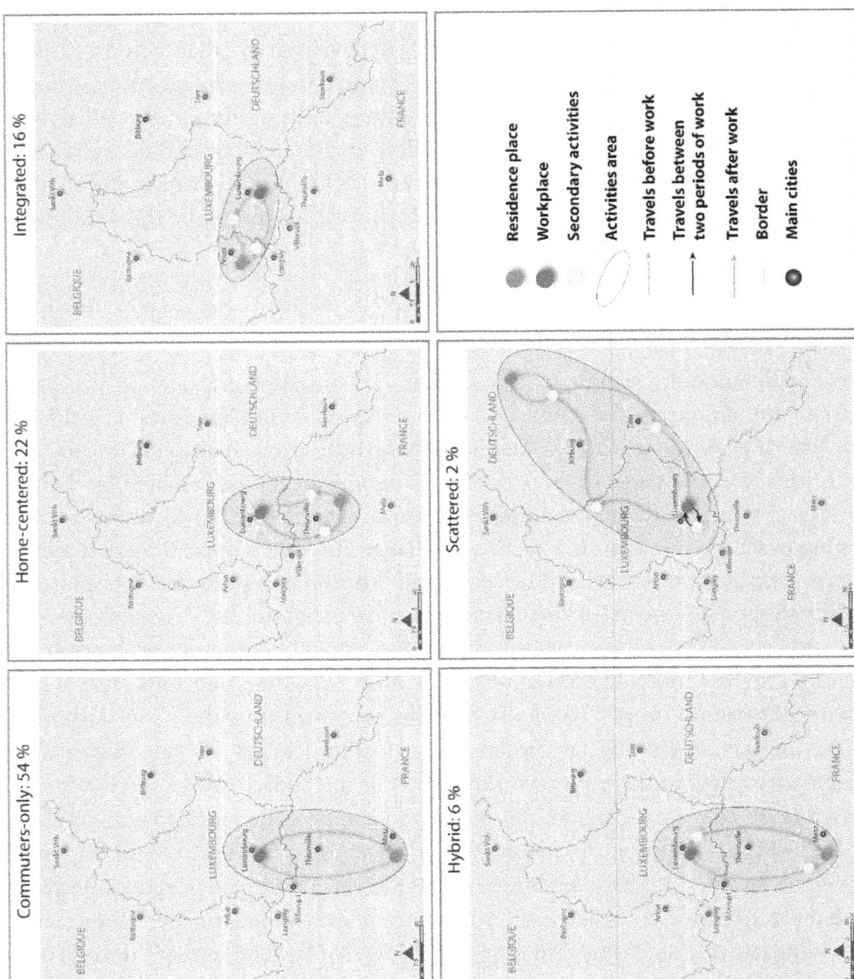

FIGURE 5.5 Examples of the Activity Space for the Five Profiles of Spatial Integration (Drevon et al., 2016)

In the case of daily cross-border workers, one can apply the same reasoning in assuming that they are torn between attachment and repulsion to their country of work. Gerber and Enaux's work (2008) on the image of residential areas of border workers in Luxembourg is particularly edifying as regards the relationship border workers have with their country of work. Based on a stratified sample of 2,470 cross-border commuters, the authors show that cross-border commuters are generally attached to their workplace, which they readily include in the representation of their living area. Attachment to the workplace is mainly linked to job satisfaction (attractive salaries) and the fact that cross-border workers tend to be born near the border. National specificities emerged, however. German cross-border workers, for instance, had a more positive transnational image due to job seniority and linguistic proximity. For Belgians, this representation was somewhat hampered by job dissatisfaction and the language barrier. French border workers' feelings were similar to those of Germans (seniority and job satisfaction). However, children attending school in the country of residence and a non-border spouse tended to favor activities in the country of residence. Thus, the relationship with "the other side" tends to fluctuate between attraction and repulsion based on complex processes linked to social, economic and cultural aspects.

In sum, urban cross-border regions are particularly interesting for understanding the opportunities and limits of the European integration process at the local level. Although they enjoy the advantages of free trade agreements (tourism, border work, trade), they also bear witness to the territorial repercussions of international European agreements, and notably in the daily lives of border populations. Border differentials, for example, impact land and real estate prices, daily mobility conditions and access to cross-border resources in general. Thus, the European agreements designed to forge and strengthen interstate cooperation were ultimately successful in anticipating repercussions at the local level. Beyond critiquing these texts and their programmatic dimension in terms of cross-border urban regions, the difficulty of anticipating or forging a real political vision lies in the geographical, social, linguistic and economic diversity of Europe's cross-border regions. This diversity, which is at the root of a number of barrier effects, helps explain the hardships that urban cross-border regions face in terms of developing different forms of commons and links that transcend the barriers inherent to such territories. One of the main challenges of building Europe is developing a policy of cooperation and integration that links the various European levels. This linking of scales cannot be forged with simple commercial and monetary agreements; rather, it is a question of building a set of commons that account for the diversity of cross-border regions economically, culturally and spatially.

Conclusion

Faced with the European Union's crisis of legitimacy, this chapter argues for an individual-centered approach to cross-border regions' integration that takes into account both the complexity of the configurations of border regions and individual behaviors, as well as the perception of the cross-border territories and their inhabitants. In this way, the chapter proposes a critical review of European cooperation processes by highlighting the uniformity of cooperation modalities that challenge the diversity of cross-border regions' configurations. We also propose a critical review of past research on classic cross-border integration, which is often oriented toward transport infrastructure and urban planning. Based on a literature review, we suggest that cooperation processes in Europe must take into account the diversity of cross-border configurations. We also propose to strengthen the individual-centred approach, which is promising in terms of understanding the dynamics that underpin social-cohesion in cross-border regions. In this chapter, we discuss four pertinent ways of constructing an individual-centered approach to improve cross-border regions' integration. In this perspective, the chapter argues for taking into account the complexity of social relations in cross-border regions as well as the multiplicity of social and territorial ties that characterize these transnational territories and make them so fertile. In this way, the chapter proposes go further by putting into perspective new approaches for understanding cross-border relations based on analyzing time spent on either side of the border, daily experiences of crossing the border and different forms of attachment to cross-border territories. These original approaches to the integration and cohesion of urban cross-border regions are likely to renew the levers of European public policies by taking into account both the lifestyles and the identities of inhabitants of cross-border regions.

References

Anderson, J. E., & van Wincoop, E. (2004). Trade costs. *Journal of Economic Literature, 42*, 691–751.

Balogh, P. (2013). Sleeping abroad but working at home: Cross-border residential mobility between transnationalism and (re)bordering. *Geografiska Annaler: Series B, Human Geography, 95*, 189–204.

Bavoux, J.-J., & Chapelon, L. (2014). *Dictionnaire d'analyse spatiale*. Paris: Armand Colin.

Cappellin, R., Batey, P. W. J., & Cappelin, T. R. (1993). *Regional networks, border regions and European integration*. London: Pion Ltd.

Drevon, G. (2016). *Mobilité quotidienne et stratégies d'adaptation spatio-temporelles des ménages: Une approche comparée des espaces transfrontaliers et non frontaliers des métropoles luxembourgeoises et grenobloises* (PhD thesis). Université Grenoble Alpes.

Drevon, G., Gerber, P., Klein, O., & Enaux, C. (2016). Measuring functional integration by identifying the trip chains and the profiles of cross-border workers: Empirical evidences from Luxembourg. *Journal of Borderlands Studies, 0*, 1–20.

Dubois, Y. (2017). Cross-border life in Europe: Daily mobility in the Trinational Metropolis of Basel. *Cuadernos Europeos de Deusto, 56-Governing Mobility in Europe: Interdisciplinary Perspectives*, 133–160.

Dubois, Y. (2019). *Frontières et mobilité au quotidien: Modes de vie dans l'agglomération trinationale de Bâle*. Neuchâtel: Alphil éditions.

Dujardin, C. (2001). Effet de frontière et interaction spatiale: Les migrations alternantes et la frontière linguistique en Belgique. *L'Espace Géographique, 30*, 307–320.

Durand, F., & Decoville, A. (2020). A multidimensional measurement of the integration between European border regions. *Journal of European Integration*, *42*, 163–178. Scopus.

Enaux, C., & Gerber, P. (2008). Les déterminants de la représentation transnationale du bassin de vie. Une approche fondée sur l'attachement au lieu des frontaliers luxembourgeois. *Revue d'Economie Regionale Urbaine, Décembre*, 725–752.

Gerber, P. (2012). Advancement in conceptualizing cross-border daily mobility: The Benelux Context in the European Union. *European Journal of Transport and Infrastructure Research*, *2*, 178–197.

Grasland, C. (1997). L'analyse des discontinuités territoriales: L'exemple de la structure par âge des régions européennes vers 1980. *L'Espace Géographique*, *26*, 309–326.

Grasland, C., & Hamez, G. (2005). Vers la construction d'un indicateur de cohésion territoriale européen ? *LEspace Geographique, tome 34*, 97–116.

Hägerstraand, T. (1970). What about people in regional science? *Papers in Regional Science*, *24*, 7–171.

Hamez, G. (2004). *Du transfrontalier au transnational: Approche géographique. L'exemple de la frontière franco-belge* (PhD thesis). Université Panthéon-Sorbonne – Paris I.

Hamez, G., Ruffray, S., Grasland, C., Lambert, N., Hamm, A., & Moron, E. (2011). *Enjeux des territoires frontaliers à l'échelle nationale: Vers la détermination et la délimitation de pôles transfrontaliers*. Paris: DATAR.

Hofstede, G. (1984). *Culture's consequences: International differences in work-related values*. Newbury Park, CA: Sage Publications.

Houtum, H. van. (2000). III European perspectives on borderlands. *Journal of Borderlands Studies*, *15*, 56–83.

Houtum, H. van. (2005). The geopolitics of borders and boundaries. *Geopolitics*, *10*, 672–679.

Mathä, T., & Wintr, L. (2009). Commuting flows across bordering regions: A note. *Applied Economics Letters*, *16*, 735–738.

Newman, D. (2003). On borders and power: A theoretical framework. *Journal of Borderlands Studies*, *18*, 13–25.

Newman, D. (2006). Borders and bordering: Towards an interdisciplinary dialogue. *European Journal of Social Theory*, *9*, 171–186.

Nijkamp, P., Rietveld, P., & Salomon, I. (1990). Barriers in spatial interactions and communications – A conceptual exploration. *The Annals of Regional Science*, *24*, 237–252.

Pattaroni, L. (2013). Mode de vie. In *Préparer la transition mobilitaire* (Forum Vies Mobiles). Paris: Forum Vies Mobiles.

Poulain, M., & Foulon, M. (1998). Frontières linguistiques, migrations et distribution spatiale des noms de famille en Belgique. *L'Espace Géographique*, *27*, 53–62.

Rietveld, P. (2012). Barrier effects of borders: Implications for border crossing infrastructures. *European Journal of Transport and Infrastructure Research*, *12*. https://doi.org/10.18757/ejtir.2012.12.2.2959

Schiebel, J., Omrani, H., & Gerber, P. (2015). Border effects on the travel mode choice of resident and cross- border workers in Luxembourg. *European Journal of Transport and Infrastructure Research*, *15*, 570–596.

Schönfelder, S., & Axhausen, K. W. (2010). *Urban rhythms and travel behaviour: Spatial and temporal phenomena of daily travel*. London: Routledge.

Sohn, C., & Stambolic, N. (2015). The urban development of European border regions: A spatial typology. *Europa Regional*, *2013*, 177–189.

Spierings, B., & Velde, M. van der (2008). Shopping, borders and unfamiliarity: Consumer mobility in Europe. *Tijdschrift Voor Economische En Sociale Geografie*, *99*, 497–505.

Spierings, B., & Velde, M. van der. (2013). Cross-border differences and unfamiliarity: Shopping mobility in the Dutch-German Rhine-Waal Euroregion. *European Planning Studies*, *21*, 5–23.

Taillefer, F. (1970). Les phénomènes de discontinuité en géographie par Roger Brunet. *Annales de Géographie*, *79*, 492–494.

Velde, M. van der. (2004). The power of cross-border labour market immobility. *Tijdschrift Voor Economische En Sociale Geografie*, *95*, 100–107.

Vickerman, R. W. (1994). The channel tunnel and regional development in Europe: An overview. *Applied Geography*, *14*, 9–25.

6

VOICES AGAINST MOBILITY

Introduction

One of the lessons to be learned from the COVID-19 crisis has been that it seems possible – and even reasonable – to restrict mobility flows in certain circumstances. Imposed lockdown, an injunction to social distancing, the closing of borders and the controlling of people's movements all reflect a situation in which mobility flows have been greatly limited. The principal motive behind these measures was the same: to reduce physical contact between people in order to curb or slow contagion within the population. While the implementation of these measures varies from one country to another, and although the scientific debate on the effects of this strategy is still open, this unprecedented limitation of mobility reminds us that ever-increasing flows and movement is not a historical constant. Of course, not all forms of mobility have been banned. In fact, certain activities, such as the transport of goods and services, have expanded, in large part due to widespread use of online shopping platforms. In short, while some forms of mobility have been deemed dangerous and therefore limitable, others seem more necessary than ever.

While the previous chapters highlighted the diversity of mobility flows and strategies for promoting them, this chapter focuses on some of the arguments used to challenge them. What are these arguments? Wherein lies the legitimacy of such a challenge? And perhaps more fundamentally even, are there common arguments and legitimacy within this opposition? This chapter seeks to answer these questions and to highlight certain commonalities. Effectively, if mobility is widely contested in certain circumstances, it is mainly due to a sense of danger or problems linked to mobility. The fact that a person, good or service is mobile can result in changes that can be perceived as a threat. As Tim Cresswell points out, mobility has often been portrayed as a threat in Western society, a bug in the system, something to be controlled (Cresswell, 2006). In some cases, and as the COVID-19 crisis has shown,

DOI: 10.4324/9780429325014-6

this threat nonetheless seems to be objective. In other cases, situations arising from the existence of a particular type of mobility (for example, migratory flows) can be subjectively perceived as a threat. The moral legitimacy of these two fears may, as it turns out, be different. Yet, the fear felt in both cases is very real.

This chapter presents four areas where opposition to mobility has emerged and converged, namely transport infrastructure and facilities, immigration flows, tourist flows and health crises. It then discusses the commonalities of different opposing positions and how they can be conceptualized as a reaction against a larger socio-infrastructure development pattern, which is described in the last section.

Opposing Mobilities

Opposition to mobility flows takes different forms. In this section, we analyse four different areas or situations where opposition to mobility exists, namely transport infrastructure and facilities, immigration flows, tourist flows and health crises.

Opposition to Transport Infrastructure

One of the most basic ways of challenging mobility is to oppose infrastructural and technical systems (specific modes of transport), which make managing flows possible. In certain cases, the argument centers on infrastructure and technical measures. In most cases, however, opposition targets these factors as well as problems generated by mobility flows. Historically speaking, transport infrastructure projects have always met staunch opposition, a phenomenon that has only intensified in recent decades. The process of "destructuring territories by networks" (Offner & Pumain, 1996, p. 23) has been widely explored based on examples in the transport field, and studies on opposition to transport infrastructure in Europe abound (Audikana, 2017; Baverez, 2011; Bobbio & Zeppetella, 2003; Della Porta & Piazza, 2008; Fillieule, 2003; Halpern, 2006; Lolive, 1999; Oosterlynck & Swyngedouw, 2010; Rui, Ollivier-Trigalo, & Fourniau, 2001). This opposition is often of the NIMBY (Not In My Back Yard) type and focuses on the potential negative effects of new infrastructure from a subjective standpoint (O'Hare & Audikana, 2017). However, and more generally, opponents to transport infrastructure also question the social, environmental and economic impacts of such projects. Thus, through a process of increasing generality, anti-transport infrastructure rhetoric has become more sophisticated and tends to systematically express opinions regarding the negative impact of mobility systems.

Our research on opposition to high-speed rail line projects incited us to study some of the different arguments advanced (Audikana & Chen, 2016). In Europe, much of the opposition to high-speed rail projects has been led by left-wing political parties, environmental groups and anti-globalization movements. The strong community identity of the anti-high-speed rail movement is a constant and necessary condition for achieving the desired objectives in Europe's case. While in certain instances the "solidarity" of this community predominantly unites home and land owners affected by the new route (Marshall, 2012; Rui, 2001), the community identity of small towns and the rural world are very much marked in others (Audikana, 2017; Della Porta & Piazza, 2008). Opponents first and foremost cite environmental problems linked to transport infrastructure. Moreover, high-speed rail is seen as responding to the needs of a hypermobile elite and is therefore not a social priority for most citizens. Finally, opponents consider that the decision-making process lacks transparency and participation when it comes to making mobility and investment choices. European opponents criticize the rationale behind such projects and advocate for new models of economic and social development. In a joint declaration (Charter of Hendaye, 2010), several groups opposed to high-speed rail described the territorial and social problems linked to this type of project:

> These projects constitute an ecological, socioeconomic and human disaster for the territories they cross . . . These projects are unable to lead to the participation of the population in decision processes . . . We oppose the aberrant expansion of transport provoked by the globalized capitalism, and which does not allow a uniform local development, but on the contrary supports abnormal concentration of the traffics and productions and a wild delocalization.

Opposition to mobility infrastructure is also highly marked at the urban level. In a study on opposition to the Cornavin station extension project in Geneva (Audikana & Kaufmann, 2016), we highlighted the existence of two diametrically opposed visions of urban development. Although based on principles of sustainable transport development, these two positions were, in many ways, antagonistic. On one hand is a metropolitan vision that considers urban development at the territorial scale and thus develop regional rail transport infrastructure that allows for the urbanization of neighborhoods surrounding stations. In this perspective, Cornavin station and the surrounding neighborhood become a central area to be densified and developed so as to create a dynamic of metropolitan-wide services and facilities (and jobs more notably). On the other hand is a vision, which was more centered on local life and supported by the neighborhood residents directly affected by the project, that emphasizes social diversity in downtown neighborhoods in the name of social cohesion and the preservation of urbanity.

Anti-Immigration Rhetoric

Historically speaking, managing migratory flows has been the crux of many forms of opposition to mobility. Migration flows are the voluntary or forced geographic movement of individuals seeking to settle in another place. This movement, which can occur between rural and urban areas, within a country or between different countries, has often been met with resistance. Different theoretical perspectives help explain such reactions (McLaren & Johnson, 2007). For instance, the arrival of new population groups can be perceived by individuals as competition for available resources in a given context. Generally speaking, this competition concerns access to jobs and housing as well as the allocation of social assistance. In certain cases, however, this competition is experienced collectively and leads to a differentiation of resources: a "we and our" whose appropriation by a "they or them" is called into question. At other times, opposition to migratory flows is closely linked to an identity-type reaction to differences in cultures, values and ways of life. The habit of associating migratory flows with an increase in crime can also be framed in this symbolic reaction to new arrivals.

Anti-immigration rhetoric often materializes in the form of mobility control measures. These measures, which aim to limit migration flows, vary (Rosière & Jones, 2012). The frontline, which is considered as an empty space between two or more zones and is a distancing measure that is used less and less, emerges naturally in certain cases. In recent decades, the Mediterranean has acted as a frontline between European and African/Middle Eastern countries by rendering the arrival of immigration flows more difficult and dangerous. Different control and surveillance measures are often implemented in areas where land masses meet (e.g., straits) in order to monitor the passage of people. This is the case in the Strait of Gibraltar in Spain, where authorities attempt to control the arrival of clandestine boats from Africa. Finally, barriers and walls are other distancing measures that, paradoxically, are being increasingly used in the current context of advanced globalization. Donald Trump's intense campaign for the construction of a wall between Mexico and the United States and images of people trying to climb over fences in Ceuta and Melilla reflect this state of affairs. Such apparatuses of control now employ new technologies, such as radars, sensors and cameras, which allow for exhaustive control of entry. In short, these different measures are designed to control the unwanted movement of people based on anti-immigration rhetoric. While the effectiveness of these measures is far from proven, their implementation symbolically fuels and reinforces this same rhetoric.

In some local contexts, and as indicated in the previous chapter, opposition to mobility flows tends to target daily cross-border commuters. While these populations cohabitate and share the same spaces (and even cultures), it turns out that this commuter presence often gives rise to a rhetoric of rejection. Switzerland is a clear example of this type of tension, with around 300,000 cross-border workers employed there but living in other countries (namely France, Italy, Germany and Austria). Cross-border commuters are often viewed negatively in areas like in Geneva and Ticino, where cross-border work is most prevalent. These individuals benefit from a Swiss job and salary but reside, socialize and consume on the other side of the border (Delaugerre, 2013). Moreover, the daily mobility generated by this type of commuting creates problems for the Swiss resident population in a geographical context where cross-border infrastructure is still limited (Herzog & Sohn, 2014). This rhetoric has been used and systematized by political forces that have made rejecting cross-border workers their hallmark.

A more recent addition to anti-immigration rhetoric is the instrumentalizing of pro-environmental arguments to contest this type of mobility. In certain cases, one recognizes a green populationist movement that decries problems linked to possible overpopulation and resource consumption, inspired by Malthusian visions (Angus, Butler, Hartmann, & Kovel, 2011). Hence, a historical analysis of the pro-demographic restriction movement in the United States reveals the converging of pro-environmental and anti-immigration positions (Hultgren, 2014). Such analyses conclude that the pro-demographic restriction rhetoric currently brandished by eco-communitarians is also used by other political traditions, such as liberal and green movements. Other analyses effectively show that environmental rhetoric has played an important role in the agendas of the anti-immigration movements of right-wing populist groups in Europe (Forchtner, 2020).

We observed such a melding of pro-environmental movements and anti-immigration rhetoric in our analyses of anti-immigration campaigns in Switzerland (Kaufmann & Audikana, 2017). In the latter, groups in favor of reducing immigration have systematically developed and used pro-environmental arguments to defend their position over the past decade. By mustering an urbanophobic vision of Switzerland (Salomon Cavin & Woeffray, 2010), these movements have seized on the country's increasing metropolization that has resulted from population growth due to an intensification of immigration. Limiting immigration is therefore necessary in order to temper urbanization in Switzerland, control energy and resource consumption and stabilize needs in terms of housing, infrastructure and facilities. Anti-urbanization rhetoric and positions have thus stoked the fires of anti-urban sentiments in Switzerland, raising environmental concerns and refueling anti-immigration arguments.

This merging of anti-immigration positions and environmental issues is revelatory of rhetorical hybridization vis-à-vis mobility. Indeed, while these areas have traditionally been treated as separate and distinct, we can see how the two issues have, in certain cases, become entangled. Thus, in a certain way, opposing immigration is a way of meeting the demands of sustainable development. The environmental agenda, in turn, seems to be concerned with how migration flows are managed. With this in mind, the argument that it is erroneous to assign mobility flows to an isolated domain advanced in this chapter seems to be partially confirmed. As we shall see, one can identify common reasons and arguments that justify opposition to cross-border worker or migrant flows with regard to the creation of new transport infrastructure. We do not ignore the utilitarian ambition that may underlie this blending of domains, especially for those who use environmental arguments to justify identity positions. However, one must recall that, even from an environmental standpoint, certain statements in favor of limiting mobility flows seem to resonate more loudly than in the past.

Overtourism and Anti-Tourist Attitudes

Over the past decade, various protest movements have emerged in opposition to the increase and intensification of tourist flows in certain cities and regions of Europe and the world. Anti-tourist sentiments are not a new phenomenon. The negative view of tourism and tensions between tourists and locals have continued to grow since the emergence of modern tourism in the 19th century (Novy & Colomb, 2016). While, historically, opposition to tourist flows has been largely unanalysed, the development of "overtourism" has recently drawn attention to the phenomenon. Overtourism can be defined as "the acceleration and growth of tourism supply and demand, the use of tourism destinations' natural ecological goods, the destruction of their cultural attractions, and the negative impacts on their social and economic environments" (Mihalic, 2020, p. 1). Unlike the intellectual anti-tourism rhetoric associated with mass tourism, contemporary disputes are directly linked to the dynamics of "overcrowding." Overcrowding refers to contexts in which popular spaces, public spaces and transport services are increasingly saturated, and new neighborhoods become new tourist destinations (Novy & Colomb, 2019). Overcrowding has deteriorated the quality of life in certain places and had a negative impact on inhabitants' conviviality. Such phenomena likewise affect the experience of visitors, who end up avoiding overcrowded destinations. The issues caused by tourist flows depend not only on the volume of flows but also the specific characteristics of these destinations (Milano, 2018). Tourist flows do not have the same impact depending on the physical and spatial conditions of a place (large city, small town, seaside areas or other natural spaces).

Certain European cities like Barcelona, Rome and Amsterdam have become clear examples of such overcrowding. The intensification of tourist flows generates a host of negative effects and externalities in urban spaces (Novy & Colomb, 2019). These effects and the benefits linked to the increase in flows are unevenly distributed among inhabitants and actors in these areas. What is more, in some cases, attracting tourist flows and creating facilities and services for the tourism sector have become priority items on the agendas and budgets of local governments. The physical impacts are typically the most obvious: traffic congestion, the deterioration of public spaces, the privatization of certain spaces for tourism purposes, the standardization of the urban landscape, environmental pressures and changes in land use. However, these physical changes go hand in hand with other types of dynamics. From an economic standpoint, for instance, these situations can lead to significant changes in local commerce with the creation of establishments geared towards tourists, the arrival of large chain stores, the disappearance of local businesses and an increase in product prices and commercial rents. Moreover, the increase in and sprawl of establishments and accommodations for tourists can also trigger processes of gentrification and the displacement of local populations. The negative effects linked to tourist flows can also produce socio-cultural changes in the areas concerned. Problems related to the uses of the urban space, the distortion of local culture, incivility and delinquency phenomena, the implementation of repressive measures and loss of diversity are realities in some cities. From a more psychological standpoint, this can result in a diminished sense of belonging and detachment from places, which gradually become unfamiliar.

The case of Barcelona is a clear example of the development and spread of an anti-tourism movement (Hughes, 2018; Ramos & Mundet, 2020). The roots of this movement lie in the city's urban renewal policy since the 1908s, which has resulted in changes in the city's productive fabric and international influence. This process has been widely criticized by certain resident groups and associations, which have suffered the direct impact of gentrification dynamics since the 1990s. It was starting in the 2010s – with lodging geared to tourists on platforms like Airbnb and the rampant increase in incivility – that this type of movement began to target the tourism industry more directly. For most movements and activists opposed to such development, the uncontrolled increase in tourist flows in the past decades fundamentally explains all of these phenomena.

Overtourism and overcrowding phenomena are often linked to greater accessibility to these cities through the development of new transport infrastructure and facilities. Barcelona, a port city, is a clear example of how cruise activities affect port cities like it and, even more so, Venice. Cruise activities are the catalyst for a variety of mobility flows (Brandajs & Russo, 2019, p. 3): "the mobility of large cruise ships into and off an urban port, the mobility of passengers boarding, disembarking or wandering into the destination mostly in organized tours, of goods and objects like provisions, luggage, tour buses and taxis, and of the capital investments and even policies that sustain the growth of cruise ports." In Barcelona, certain public areas seem to be completely saturated by streams of cruise ship guests. City residents tend to avoid these areas, even outside of peak times.

In Venice, opposition to overtourism is indeed organized but instead targets cruise ships themselves as a mode of transport. The city has maintained its tourist attractiveness despite continued "overcrowding," but daily uses and perception of intangible heritage have changed profoundly (Bertocchi & Visentin, 2019). Cruise ship traffic increased in Venice in the 2000s with the development of new infrastructures (Vianello, 2018). It was with the arrival and proliferation of large cruises that the opposition group Comitato No Grandi Navi – Laguna Bene Comune (No Big Ships – the Lagoon as a Common Good) was founded. This group advocates for banning large cruise ships from navigating in the Venice lagoon. It also criticizes the investments in the heavy infrastructure needed to accommodate them, the risks associated with their presence and their role in the "overcrowding" of the city more generally. The case of Venice is an interesting example in that opposition to different types of mobility tends to overlap. Opposition to large infrastructure and the transport system associated with the cruise sector (No Big Ships) has thus become a way of contesting the logic of increased tourist flows. In this case, opposition to the infrastructure symbolizes the rejection of a development model that involves saturating spaces due to an exponential increase in mobility flows.

Social Distanciation and Mobility Restrictions

The implementation of social distancing and mobility restrictions were some of the key measures adopted by different governments to deal with the spread of COVID-19 both in Europe and in other regions of the world in 2020. In terms of pandemic management, mobility is also considered a dynamic that must be limited in order to reduce the risk of infection or, at the very least, lower its spread rate. Public health goals appear to be a priority when it comes to adopting and justifying restrictive measures. The debate on the actual benefits of these measures and the economic and social effects associated with them is undoubtedly far from over (Bialasiewicz & Eckes, 2020; Espinoza, Castillo-Chavez, & Perrings, 2020; Kraemer et al., 2020).

Similar measures have been implemented in the past to deal with other diseases and epidemiological phenomena (Giles-Vernick, Craddock, & Gunn, 2010). Three notable examples are: quarantine, which isolates healthy people who have been in contact with a given pathogen; isolation, which aims to set the sick apart from the rest of the population; and mobility restrictions, which are measures that limit access to certain spaces or geographic perimeters by certain individuals or groups. These measures are part of a biosecurity strategy that aims to regulate circulation. However, it is important to distinguish between good movement, which should be encouraged, and that involving health risks, which should be controlled and limited (Bingham & Hinchliffe, 2008). The role of cities, and global cities more specifically, as places of interconnection and dissemination of viruses and other threats has been stressed by certain analysts (Ali & Keil, 2008).

We do not currently have the hindsight to understand all of the effects and the full significance of the COVID-19 pandemic. However, in practice, it seemed necessary to adopt extreme measures to limit mobility flows, at least during the most acute phases. This has radically changed our perception of a world doomed to boundless hypermobility. The pandemic has thus confirmed a certain hypothesis: the spread and intensification of mobility flows over the past decades, which have allowed for greater interconnection and proximity between individuals at the global scale, have also laid the foundations for systemic fragility linked to this gain in accessibility. Being "accessible" so as to offer the benefits of globalization bears certain risks; nowadays, we are obliged to neutralize this mobility and limit accessibility to reduce risks and restore security.

Commonalities Against Mobility

In this chapter we have attempted to identify the areas in which rhetoric in opposition to mobility has emerged and consolidated. The underlying hypothesis was to consider that, despite the variety of situations and approaches used, certain arguments against mobility follow a similar logic. Can we conclude from this that opposition to high-speed trains, attempts to limit migrant flows to or from a country, blocking access to certain urban areas to groups of tourists or the decision to lockdown an entire continent are comparable situations? Probably not, but it is nonetheless interesting to identify the underlying rationales, which seem to be shared in these different situations, while highlighting the interactions and contradictions between these different anti-mobility logics.

One common key element of these rationales is associating mobility flows with a risk or threat. This fact has often been raised by mobility theorists. Cresswell (Cresswell, 2006, p. 26), for example, points out that one of the main ways of thinking about mobility "is to see it as a threat, a disorder in the system, a thing to control." In the areas we have just explored, opponents of mobility flows effectively consider their variation, increase and even their very existence to be a threat. As we have seen, the arguments used vary greatly from one context to another (environmental concerns, economic competition, sociability-related reasons, the loss of place/cultural identity, health-related reasons, etc.). Each argument tends to focus on a particular area. Environmental arguments, for example, are therefore widely used to oppose transport infrastructure, while identity-type arguments are more often used when questions of immigration are at stake.

However, more interesting are the situations in which arguments or domains merge. Two interesting cases in this regard are the adopting of pro-environment arguments to justify anti-immigration measures (Switzerland is a clear example in this regard) and mobilization against "overtourism" (in the form of opposition to infrastructure or facilities associated with increased tourist flows). Venice inhabitants' opposition to the presence of cruise ships is an example of this: resistance to infrastructure policy rejects the development model directly associated with maximizing tourist flows. We consider that such hybridizing of arguments and domains will only continue in the future, thus highlighting situations in which mobility is perceived as a threat. The COVID-19 health crisis shows how distancing measures and mobility restrictions can justify less ambitious transport investments at specific times, given the possible reemergence of new health risks in the future.

Of course, the notion of risk or threat and the arguments used can controversial. The question is whether this risk or threat can be measured objectively or not, and, if not, whose perception and values they reflect. We can conclude that in most of the cases described, even those that seem incontestably objective (i.e., a threat), subjective perception nonetheless plays a key role.

However, beyond the more or less subjective and constructed nature of these situations, what seems clear is that the ability to protect oneself against risks or threats differs among individuals and groups. While we can easily take a critical stance vis-à-vis anti-immigration discourse, it is more difficult to deny that migration flows (in terms of competition for jobs, for example) do not impact the entire population the same way. Similarly, gentrification processes linked to increased tourist flows are, by definition, a dynamic that excludes and marginalizes a certain portion of inhabitants. Faced with a perceived risk associated with the building of new infrastructure, some groups and individuals may take protective measures (including the decision to relocate) that others cannot afford. Even in the case of the COVID-19 health crisis, one can assume that older people would favor more restrictive mobility measures due to increased health risks for that population. Ultimately, the possible effects of different mobility situations are not distributed equally among the population. From this, we can gather that some groups and individuals have more reasons to oppose the perceived risk or threat presented by mobility than others.

Another key element that emerges from this analysis is the fact that opposition to mobility seems to prevail in situations where promoting mobility has become an objective in itself for public authorities and certain private actors. This radical vision of the benefits of mobility beyond any other principle or objective has often led to the silencing or ignoring of critiques that question this hierarchy of values in favor of mobility. When protest movements do emerge, they tend to argue for redefining mobility not as an objective in itself, but rather as an element for achieving other values or goals. By reprioritising mobility arguments (versus the idea of "free mobility without conditions"), we can better manage different types of mobility while being aware of the harm it can cause.

In such instances, when opposition to mobility does bring about change, it generally does not involve a total restriction of mobility but rather measures to better regulate flows. Mobility, in this case, is but one ingredient among others to take into account when it comes to acting in our societies, and not necessarily the final objective. Reducing or limiting mobility in terms of speed limits, traffic volumes or social distancing is thus, in some case, not only understandable, but even reasonable. Once again, in order to enrich this debate, it is essential to consider the various arguments and objectives (besides mobility). While the latter seem to be given higher priority than excessive defense of mobility, measures to limit mobility will be seen as more legitimate and, in some cases, be put into practice. All of this requires greater attention and sensitivity to the negatively perceived effects of mobility and their distribution.

A Critique of the Socio-Infrastructure Mega-Development Model

We hypothesize that the forms of opposition described in this chapter are intrinsically associated with a specific social development model. More precisely, drawing on critical social theory (Brenner, 2004; Harvey, 2001; Rosa, 2013; J. C. Scott, 1998; Swyngedouw, Moulaert, & Rodriguez, 2002), we associate the emergence of this opposition to a socio-infrastructure development logic characterized by economic accumulation, political centralization, spatial concentration and temporal acceleration. This development logic is structured around the idea of megaprojects.

Megaprojects can be defined as "large-scale, complex ventures that . . . take many years to develop and build, involve multiple public and private stakeholders, are transformational, and impact millions of people" (Flyvbjerg, 2017, p. 2). There are typically four such types (Gellert & Lynch, 2003, p. 16): infrastructure (transport, energy, water, sewer, information technology, etc.); extraction (minerals, oil, gas, etc.); production (industrial processing plants, export processing zones, manufacturing parks, etc.); and consumption (mega-events, massive tourist installations, real estate developments, etc.).

Beyond their size, megaprojects are characterized by their transformational (Flyvbjerg, 2017, p. 2), trait-making (Hirschman, 2015, p. xix), disruptive (Altshuler & Luberoff, 2003, p. 2), dream-creating (Söderlund, Sankaran, & Biesenthal, 2017, p. 6) or, more radically, creative-destructive (Gellert & Lynch, 2003, p. 15) ambitions. Megaprojects are not only conceived as solutions to meet global needs and challenges (W. R. Scott, 2011; Söderlund et al., 2017) but also as drivers of development and change. To describe the "anatomy" (Flyvbjerg, Bruzelius, & Rothengatter, 2003, p. subtitle) of such ambition, Flyvbjerg (2014, pp. 8–9) identifies four "sublimes," which explain the appeal of megaprojects: 1) the technological sublime, or engineers' excitement at building large and innovative projects; 2) the political sublime, or politicians' desire to build visible monuments to themselves and their causes; 3) the economic sublime, or the expectation of profits shared by the economic actors involved in the implementation of megaprojects; and 4) the aesthetic sublime, which attracts designers interested in iconic projects. The combination of these sublimes ensures strong coalitions among "stakeholders who benefit from megaprojects and will therefore work for more such projects" (Flyvbjerg, 2014, p. 9).

Megaprojects are capital-intensive endeavours, and their construction prioritizes interventions that attract investments that reinforce the same logic, leading to an accumulation of resources in a specific sector. Megaprojects are risky and require a centralized political authority to provide assurance to investors, above and beyond the regulatory capacity of the multiple jurisdictions potentially affected by the project. Megaprojects are "spatially situated" (Gellert & Lynch, 2003, p. 15) and transform space, concentrating activities and population in spaces that are already intensively used. They transform the way time is experienced and contribute to social acceleration by facilitating communication, mobility and exchange. These common features make megaprojects a distinctive subset of development interventions. They have the capacity to change the way we think about the world and its future. We hypothesize that the socio-infrastructure mega-development model is critical for understanding opposition to different mobilities described in this chapter. The spatial and temporal concentration of migratory, tourism and virus-related flows have in many cases led to saturated situations against which different discourses and political traditions, ranging from nationalistic to environmentalist views, have been mobilized. We argue that this situation is in contrast with the reticular (Castells, 1996), liquid (Bauman, 2000) and mobile (Urry, 2000) social worlds that were foreseen in the late 1990s. In these conceptualizations, the generalization of new technologies and communication and transport infrastructure at the global level was considered an opportunity for more horizontal social relationships and increasing social change. Instead, new communication capacities have, in many cases, led rather to saturation.

Social acceleration is a major trend in the mega-development model. The increases in travel speed made possible by modern transport technologies is a critical factor of this acceleration (Harvey, 1989; Virilio, 1977). The development of this speed has radically changed the spatial organization of societies at both the local and global levels and has also created new mobility patterns. Cities have undergone a "transition" (Wiel, 1999) from pedestrian to motorized mobility systems and urban rhythms (Amin & Thrift, 2012; Henckel, Pahl-Weber, & Herkommer, 2007; Henckel, Thomaier, Könecke, Zedda, & Stabilini, 2013; Lefebvre, 2004), and the pace of life (Bornstein & Bornstein, 1976; Levine, 1997; Levine & Norenzayan, 1999; Walmsley & Lewis, 1989; Wirtz & Ries, 1992) has been radically transformed. Speed is not, however, homogenously distributed across society. Different factors, such as accessibility to different transport systems and the timing and location of activities, can influence individuals' travel speed. The existence of such different speeds cannot be considered a social inequality in itself, since speed and mobility can also depend on personal choices and not only on external constraints. However, we hypothesize that differences in travel speed persist and can be considered an indicator of social inequality among others.

It was notably Ivan Illich in his work "Energy and Equity" (1974) who established a direct link between speed and social inequality. In a context of an international energy crisis, Illich considered that increasing energy consumption and mechanical power led to higher levels of social inequality. In his words, even "if non-polluting power were feasible and abundant, the use of energy on a massive scale acts on society like a drug that is physically harmless but psychically enslaving" (ibid., p. 6). As a result, Illich advocates for a "minimum energy economy" (ibid., p. 9) and the identification of "the thresholds beyond which power corrupts," since "only a ceiling on energy use can lead to social relations that are characterized by high levels of equity" (ibid., p. 5). Illich was thus concerned about the effects of the "escalation of capital-intensive institutional growth" (ibid., p. 8) not only in terms of physical destruction, but also in terms of social disintegration.

In order to illustrate "the more general point of socially optimal energy use" (ibid., p. 12), Illich introduced the question of traffic, defined as "any movement of people from one place to another" (ibid., p. 15) outside the home. For Illich, increasing energy consumption was correlated to increased traffic speed, which, in turn, resulted in higher levels of social inequality. A distinction was made between transit and transport as the two aspects of traffic. Transit refers to movements based on "human metabolic energy" (ibid., p. 15) (mainly walking and riding a bike), while transport refers to motorized mobility. For Illich, the former contributes to social equality since "people on their feet are more or less equal" (ibid., p. 16). On the other hand, Illich considered that motorized mobility "has reduced equality among men, restricted their mobility to a system of industrially defined routes and created time scarcity of unprecedented severity" (ibid., p. 16). More precisely, the increase in speed brought about by motorized mobility benefits only a minority while imposing a high cost for the vast majority. In Illich's words, "the marginal utility of an increment in the speed of a small number of people has for its price the growing marginal disutility of this acceleration for the great majority" (ibid., p. 30). It is in this context that Illich affirms "tell me how fast you go and I'll tell you who you are" (ibid., p. 32). In parallel, transport industries create a "radical monopoly" that, by promoting "the compulsory consumption" of motorized mobility, restricts "the conditions for enjoying an abundant use value" related to "the innate capacity for transit" (ibid., pp. 45–46). Not only are inequalities growing, but former transients are also becoming "captive consumers of transport" (ibid., p. 48).

In Illich's view, differences in speed levels are not merely an indicator of social inequality but are also a source of inequality in itself. Illich presents high speed as an environmentally harmful and socially destructive component of industrially advanced societies. Acceleration is synonymous with inequality and social slavery, and neither the public or private nature of the transport mode nor technical improvements are considered critical factors when dealing with the energetic and social effects of mobility. On the contrary, for Illich, "speed is the critical factor which makes transportation socially destructive" (ibid., p. 12). In this regard, a "sufficiently limited maximum speed" (ibid., p. 69) can contribute to greater equality and social liberation.

In this view, criticism of the problems linked to mobility, the questioning of infrastructure projects and the emergence of alternative development models are, for example, the cornerstones of the Slow movement. The Slow movement began in Italy in the late 1980s in response to the relentless acceleration of lifestyles (Rosa, 2013). Its roots come from the Slow Food movement, forged by a group of activists who came together to condemn unhealthy eating habits resulting from fast food culture, the homogenization of tastes and industrial/de-territorialized agricultural production. These activists militate for a return to local agriculture, local products and the "slow" philosophy, which respects seasonal and natural rhythms (Deléage, 2014). The Slow movement was at the heart of the Slow City concept, whose activity began in the 2000s. Through the international Cittàslow network, almost 200 small towns of less than 50,000 inhabitants have embarked on a strategy that aims to promote – among other things – the quality of the environment and urban fabric, local products and local specificity, and a sense of community (Knox, 2005). The fundamental idea is to slow down flows, production rates, etc., in order to create the conditions necessary for sustainable urban development (Turkseven Dogrusoy & Dalgakiran, 2011). While speed has long been considered a symbol of productivity and technical progress (Kaufmann, 2014), slowness now appears to be an alternative for bringing about a new urban transition (Wiel, 1999). In sum, through opposition to transport infrastructures and the nuisances related to social acceleration, the slow movement proposes alternative development models in which mobility's central role is largely questioned.

Conclusion

This chapter has described several areas (transport infrastructure and facilities, immigration flows, tourist flows and health crises) in which different types of opposition have emerged and intensified against growing mobility flows over the past decades. To be sure, this opposition cannot be considered new; rather, it is grounded in different political traditions (environmentalism, nationalism, anti-capitalism, hygienism, etc.), which have in turn addressed similar mobility-related issues. They share a similar diagnostic, in which mobility appears as a threat or risk that can negatively affect the environment, national unity, local communities and/or collective health, while their moral justification varies largely from one opposing position to another. We also identified specific situations in which the areas of opposition seem to merge. Opposition to migration flows can be structured on the environmental issues that a larger population generates in terms of mobility and land use. Similarly, opposition to major infrastructure can be criticized, as it is considered a generator of overtourism. We have argued that all of these variegated forms of opposition must be theoretically associated with a socio-infrastructure mega-development model in which large facilities and events play an increasingly important role in our societies. The EU is, in this way, an interesting laboratory in which this type of development model has been put in practice, as we indicated in Chapter 3. It is through the critique of this model that mobility opposition can provide alternative models or, at least, policy measures to manage situations in which mobility flows seem to be increasingly out of control.

References

Ali, S. H., & Keil, R. (Eds.). (2008). *Networked disease: Emerging infections in the global city*. Malden, MA: Wiley-Blackwell.

Altshuler, A. A., & Luberoff, D. (2003). *Mega-projects: The changing politics of urban public investment*. Washington, DC: Brookings Institution Press; Lincoln Institute of Land Policy.

Amin, A., & Thrift, N. J. (2012). *Cities: Reimagining the urban* (Repr). Cambridge: Polity Press.

Angus, I., Butler, S., Hartmann, B., & Kovel, J. (2011). *Too many people: Population, immigration, and the environmental crisis*. Chicago: Haymarket Books.

Audikana, A. (2017). *La politisation des trains à grande vitesse en Espagne (1986–2011): Le Léviathan n'était qu'une sirène*. Paris: L'Harmattan.

Audikana, A., & Chen, Z. (2016). For the power, against the power: The political discourses of high-speed rail in Europe, the United States and China. In M. Endres, K. Manderscheid, & C. Mincke (Eds.), *The mobilities paradigm: Discourses and ideologies* (pp. 163–185). London: Routledge.

Audikana, A., & Kaufmann, V. (2016). De la "valeur des échelles" aux "échelles de valeur": Controverses et compromis autour de l'extension de la gare Cornavin à Genève (2008–2015). *Sud-Ouest Européen, n° 40*, 141–152.

Bauman, Z. (2000). *Liquid modernity*. Cambridge, UK: Polity Press.

Baverez, N. (2011). *Assises du ferroviaire: Rapport de la commission 3 – L'économie du ferroviaire*. Ministère de l'écologie, du développement durable, des transports et du logement.

Bertocchi, D., & Visentin, F. (2019). "The overwhelmed city": Physical and social overcapacities of global tourism in Venice. *Sustainability*, *11*, 6937.

Bialasiewicz, L., & Eckes, C. (2020). 'Individual sovereignty' in pandemic times – A contradiction in terms? *Political Geography*, 102277.

Bingham, N., & Hinchliffe, S. (2008). Mapping the multiplicities of biosecurity. In A. Lakoff & S. Collier (Eds.), *Biosecurity interventions* (pp. 173–194). New York: Columbia University Press.

Bobbio, L., & Zeppetella, A. (2003). *Perché proprio qui? Grandi opere e opposizioni locali*. Milano: Franco Angeli.

Bornstein, M. H., & Bornstein, H. G. (1976). The pace of life. *Nature*, *259*, 557–559.

Brandajs, F., & Russo, A. P. (2019). Whose is that square? Cruise tourists' mobilities and negotiation for public space in Barcelona. *Applied Mobilities*, 1–25.

Brenner, N. (2004). *New state spaces: Urban governance and the rescaling of statehood*. Oxford: Oxford University Press.

Castells, M. (1996). *The rise of the network society*. Malden, MA: Blackwell Publishers.

Charter of Hendaye. (2010). *Charter of Hendaye: Joint declaration of 23 January 2010.* Retrieved from www.presidioeuropa.net/blog/charte-hendaye-la-carta-di-hendaye-la-charte-dhendaye/

Cresswell, T. (2006). *On the move: Mobility in the modern Western world.* New York: Routledge.

Delaugerre, J.-B. (2013). Être frontalier en Suisse: Le cas du canton de Genève. In R. Belkacem & I. Pigeron-Piroth (Eds.), *Le travail frontalier au sein de la Grande région Saar-Lor-Lux: Pratiques, enjeux et perspectives* (pp. 237–253). Nancy: Presses universitaires de Nancy.

Deléage, E. (2014). Le mouvement slow food: Contretemps de l'accélération temporelle? *Ecologie Politique, N°48*, 49–59.

Della Porta, D., & Piazza, G. (2008). *Voices of the valley, voices of the straits: How protest creates communities.* Oxford: Berghahn Books.

Espinoza, B., Castillo-Chavez, C., & Perrings, C. (2020). Mobility restrictions for the control of epidemics: When do they work? *PLOS ONE, 15*, e0235731.

Fillieule, O. (2003). Local environmental politics in France: Case of the Louron valley, 1984–1996. *French Politics, 1*, 305–330.

Flyvbjerg, B. (2014). What you should know about megaprojects and why: An overview. *Project Management Journal, 45*, 6–19.

Flyvbjerg, B. (2017). Introduction: The iron law of megaproject management. In *The Oxford handbook of megaproject management* (pp. 1–18). Oxford and New York: Oxford University Press.

Flyvbjerg, B., Bruzelius, N., & Rothengatter, W. (2003). *Megaprojects and risk: An anatomy of ambition.* Cambridge: Cambridge University Press.

Forchtner, B. (Ed.). (2020). *The far right and the environment: Politics, discourse and communication.* London: Routledge.

Gellert, P. K., & Lynch, B. D. (2003). Mega-projects as displacements. *International Social Science Journal, 55*, 15–25.

Giles-Vernick, T., Craddock, S., & Gunn, J. (2010). Mobility restrictions, isolation and quarantine: Historical perspectives on contemporary debates. In S. Craddock, J. Gunn, & T. Giles-Vernick (Eds.), *Influenza and public health: Learning from past pandemics* (pp. 212–231). London: Routledge.

Halpern, C. (2006). *La décision publique entre intérêt général et intérêts territorialisés: Les conflits autour de l'extension des aéroports Paris-Charles de Gaulle et Berlin-Schönefeld* (Thèse de doctorat). Institut d'études politiques, Paris, France.

Harvey, D. (1989). *The condition of postmodernity: An enquiry into the origins of cultural change.* Cambridge, MA: Blackwell.

Harvey, D. (2001). *Spaces of capital: Towards a critical geography.* New York: Routledge.

Henckel, D., Pahl-Weber, E., & Herkommer, B. (Eds.). (2007). *Time, space, places.* Frankfurt am Main: Lang.

Henckel, D., Thomaier, S., Könecke, B., Zedda, R., & Stabilini, S. (Eds.). (2013). *Space – Time design of the public city.* Dordrecht: Springer Netherlands.

Herzog, L. A., & Sohn, C. (2014). The cross-border metropolis in a global age: A conceptual model and empirical evidence from the US – Mexico and European border regions. *Global Society, 28*, 441–461.

Hirschman, A. O. (2015). *Development projects observed.* Washington, DC: Brookings Institution Press.

Hughes, N. (2018). 'Tourists go home': Anti-tourism industry protest in Barcelona. *Social Movement Studies, 17*, 471–477.

Hultgren, J. (2014). The "Nature" of American immigration restrictionism. *New Political Science, 36*, 52–75.

Illich, I. (1974). *Energy and equity.* London: Calder & Boyars.

Kaufmann, V. (2014). *Retour sur la ville mobilité et transformations urbaines*. Lausanne: Presses polytechniques et universitaires romandes.

Kaufmann, V., & Audikana, A. (2017). *Mobilité et libre circulation en Europe: Un regard suisse*. Paris: Economica.

Knox, P. L. (2005). Creating ordinary places: Slow cities in a fast world. *Journal of Urban Design, 10*, 1–11.

Kraemer, M. U. G., Yang, C.-H., Gutierrez, B., Wu, C.-H., Klein, B., Pigott, D. M., . . . Scarpino, S. V. (2020). The effect of human mobility and control measures on the COVID-19 epidemic in China. *Science, 368*, 493–497.

Lefebvre, H. (2004). *Rhythmanalysis: Space, time, and everyday life*. London: Continuum.

Levine, R. (1997). *A geography of time: The temporal misadventures of a social psychologist, or how every culture keeps time just a little bit differently*. Oxford: Oneworld.

Levine, R., & Norenzayan, A. (1999). The pace of life in 31 countries. *Journal of Cross-Cultural Psychology, 30*, 178–205.

Lolive, J. (1999). *Les contestations du TGV Méditerranée: Projet, controverse et espace public*. Paris: L'Harmattan.

Marshall, T. (2012). *Planning major infrastructure: A critical analysis*. London: Routledge.

McLaren, L., & Johnson, M. (2007). Resources, group conflict and symbols: Explaining anti-immigration hostility in Britain. *Political Studies, 55*, 709–732.

Mihalic, T. (2020). Conceptualising overtourism: A sustainability approach. *Annals of Tourism Research, 84*, 103025.

Milano, C. (2018). Overtourism, malestar social y turismofobia. Un debate controvertido. *PASOS. Revista de Turismo y Patrimonio Cultural, 18*, 551–564.

Novy, J., & Colomb, C. (2016). Urban tourism and its discontents. An introduction. In C. Colomb & J. Novy (Eds.), *Protest and resistance in the tourist city* (pp. 1–30). London and New York: Routledge.

Novy, J., & Colomb, C. (2019). Urban tourism as a source of contention and social mobilisations: A critical review. *Tourism Planning & Development, 16*, 358–375.

Offner, J.-M., & Pumain, D. (Eds.). (1996). *Réseaux et territoires: Significations croisées*. La Tour d'Aigues: Editions de l'Aube.

O'Hare, M., & Audikana, A. (2017). NIMBY reactions to HSR Conflicts over the proposed right of way. In B. L. Pérez Henríquez & E. Deakin (Eds.), *High-speed rail and sustainability decision-making and the political economy of investment* (pp. 323–336). New York: Routledge.

Oosterlynck, S., & Swyngedouw, E. (2010). Noise reduction: The postpolitical quandary of night flights at Brussels airport. *Environment and Planning A, 42*, 1577–1594.

Ramos, S. P., & Mundet, L. (2020). Tourism-phobia in Barcelona: Dismantling discursive strategies and power games in the construction of a sustainable tourist city. *Journal of Tourism and Cultural Change*, 1–19.

Rosa, H. (2013). *Social acceleration: A new theory of modernity*. New York: Columbia University Press.

Rosière, S., & Jones, R. (2012). Teichopolitics: Re-considering globalisation through the role of walls and fences. *Geopolitics, 17*, 217–234.

Rui, S. (2001). *Conflits d'aménagement, débat public et construction de l'intérêt général: Une expérience démocratique ?* (These de doctorat, Bordeaux 2). Bordeaux 2.

Rui, S., Ollivier-Trigalo, M., & Fourniau, J.-M. (2001). *Évaluer, débattre ou négocier l'utilité publique ? Identités et légitimités plurielles. Ateliers de bilan du débat publics*. Arcueil: INRETS.

Salomon Cavin, J., & Woeffray, B. (2010). L'épouvantail urbain, motif de l'aménagement du territoire en Suisse. In J. Salomon Cavin & B. Marchand (Eds.), *Antiurbain: Origines et conséquences de l'urbanophobie*. Lausanne: Presses polytechniques et universitaires romandes.

Scott, J. C. (1998). *Seeing like a state: How certain schemes to improve the human condition have failed*. New Haven: Yale University Press.

Scott, W. R. (2011). Introduction: Studying global projects. In W. R. Scott, R. E. Levitt, & R. J. Orr (Eds.), *Global projects: Institutional and political challenges* (pp. 1–12). Cambridge: Cambridge University Press.

Söderlund, J., Sankaran, S., & Biesenthal, C. (2017). The past and present of megaprojects. *Project Management Journal, 48*, 5–16.

Swyngedouw, E., Moulaert, F., & Rodriguez, A. (2002). Neoliberal urbanization in Europe: Large – scale urban development projects and the new urban policy. *Antipode, 34*, 542–577.

Turkseven Dogrusoy, I., & Dalgakiran, A. (2011). An alternative approach in sustainable planning: Slow urbanism. *Archnet-IJAR, 5*. https://doi.org/10.26687/archnet-ijar.v5i1.223

Urry, J. (2000). *Sociology beyond societies: Mobilities for the twenty-first century*. London and New York: Routledge.

Vianello, M. (2018). The "No Grandi Navi" campaign. Protests against cruise tourism in Venice. In Claire Colomb & J. Novy (Eds.), *Protest and resistance in the tourist city* (pp. 171–190). London: Routledge Taylor & Francis Group.

Virilio, P. (1977). *Vitesse et politique: Essai de dromologie*. Paris: Galilée.

Walmsley, D. J., & Lewis, G. J. (1989). The pace of pedestrian flows in cities. *Environment and Behavior, 21*, 123–150.

Wiel, M. (1999). *La Transition urbaine: Ou le passage de la ville pédestre à la ville motorisée*. Sprimont: Editions Mardaga.

Wirtz, P., & Ries, G. (1992). The pace of life – reanalysed: Why does walking speed of pedestrians correlate with city size? *Behaviour, 123*, 77–83.

7

THE SWISS EXPERIENCE

An Advanced Laboratory for Mobility Policies

Introduction

Due to its size, geographical position, and international prominence, Switzerland is an advanced laboratory for the study of mobility-related issues and policies. The Swiss context is characterized by a marked level of international openness as regards the mobility of objects, capital and services – a stark contrast to policies to limit mobility and urbanization processes at the national level. The country is likewise subject to strong immigration and cross-border flows. As such, the Swiss context favors the emergence of innovative political initiatives and policy solutions in the area of mobility. This chapter analyses Switzerland's experience in regulating mobility and tensions regarding the European framework via bilateral agreements and is based on empirical fieldwork carried out in Switzerland.

How to Govern Mobilities?

Switzerland is particularly fertile ground for exploring political controversies surrounding mobility – be it relative to the free movement of people, goods and capital – for several reasons. For one, geographically speaking, the country is located at the heart of the European continent. It also has a strongly globalized economy and a cosmopolitan society. Constitutionally speaking, it enjoys the rights of referendum and popular initiative, which allow citizens to challenge decisions taken by parliament and request a popular vote on ad-hoc proposals (by collecting citizens' signatures) respectively. These rights exist at the national, regional (canton) and municipal levels.

It was through this process of direct democracy that, on February 9, 2014, Switzerland accepted the popular initiative known as "against mass immigration." With a 55% participation rate, it was approved by 50.3% of voters.

DOI: 10.4324/9780429325014-7

The reaction was one of stupor and resulted in the questioning of bilateral agreements between Switzerland and the EU, especially concerning the free movement of people. Faced with the vote results and Switzerland's refusal to apply the protocol to extend the Free Movement of Persons Agreement to Croatia, the EU suspended Swiss participation in European academic research and mobility programs.

The malaise was palpable because, beyond a mere vote in a political climate specific to Switzerland, it said something about Europe in general, its construction and the tensions pervading it. Mobility is now at the heart of a number of challenges that contemporary European societies are currently facing. The February 2014 Swiss vote was but a local expression of a series of structural upheavals that can be felt across the European continent.

The acceptance of the "against mass immigration" popular initiative also reveals a paradox as, on that same day, February 9, 2014, a federal decree to invest 6.4 billion Swiss Francs to "guarantee sustainable financing for the operation, maintenance and development of railway infrastructure" was approved by 62% of voters. While the popular "against mass immigration" initiative aimed to regulate people's mobility in general and migratory flows to Switzerland more specifically, the second measure expresses a clear desire to increase the country's mobility potential. In other words, faced with two mobility issues on the same day, the majority of Swiss citizens expressed two different opinions by saying "yes" to "less mobility" and "yes" to "more mobility."

The Swiss vote and its impact raise an essential question: how to govern mobility in its various forms? To address this question, we interviewed national representatives of the five main Swiss parliamentary parties, namely: the Christian Democratic Party (PDC), the Radical Liberal Party (PLR), the Socialist Party (PS), the Democratic Union of the Centre (UDC) and the Green Party. Verbatim extracts of the interviews are cited throughout the text. We have chosen to anonymize them, as the goal is to identify fundamental political conflicts and controversies relating to mobility, not to reproduce partisan debates.

Presented in four main sections, this chapter explores the free movement of goods, people and capital. It also retraces and discusses Swiss policies in these different areas, which are often punctuated by referendums and popular initiatives. The latter help in identifying specific political positions relative to mobility, which will be summarized in the conclusion of this chapter.

The Gotthard Tunnel

In a work on the history of the Gotthard, historian Arthur Wyss-Niederer (1979) asserts that the Gotthard was not only the cradle but also one of the founding elements of the Confederation. In the 13th century, the Gotthard became a transit route thanks to the opening of the upper portion of the Schöllenen Gorge, at which point control became an issue: the pass and neighboring valleys emerged from their 1000-year isolation and were exposed to the harsh light of political rivalries. Faced with the power of the Habsburgs and their claim over the Gotthard

Mountains, the three original Swiss cantons concluded the Perpetual Alliance. The area thus became both the nucleus and the backbone of the young Confederation. One the on hand, the Gotthard is a symbol of both Swiss independence from external interference and a major communication thoroughfare. On the other hand, it symbolizes the connecting and structuring of the European territory. It was born to face Europe, and yet was at its service. The author concludes by saying that the Via Helvetica of yesterday and today is the Via Europaea of tomorrow.

June 1st, 2016

The Gotthard entered a new phase of its history on June 1, 2016. At 57 km, the Gotthard Tunnel became the longest rail tunnel in the world and part of the new rail line across the Alps (NLFA). It included two north-south rail lines. The project for the construction of the new transversal Alpine railway lines was approved by referendum in 1992.

The implementation of the NLFA is inseparable from the Europeanist position adopted by the Federal Council in the late 1980s (Miéville, 2013), which culminated in May 1992 with the signing of the European Economic Area (EEA) agreement and, at Switzerland's request, the opening of negotiations with a view to joining Europe. Although the Federal Council noted that it was no longer urgent to build new cross-sections of the Alpine railways, new studies were launched starting in 1986. Some observers considered that Switzerland was challenged in its age-old role as a European traffic hub in a context of increasing pressure from the European Community to free and intensify trade and the development of high-speed rail networks in the three neighboring countries (Bovy, 1989). As historian Arthur Wyss-Niederer (1979, p. 201) suggested with regard to the Gotthard ten years earlier, the decision to build the NLFA should be seen as Switzerland's participation in European politics:

> If Switzerland agrees to modernize this artery at the cost of considerable sacrifices and because it feels morally committed to it, then its participation in European politics will not have been an empty word.

In 1992, in the agreement between the Confederation and the European Economic Community on the transport of goods by road and rail, Switzerland committed to building the NFLA, a commitment that was confirmed by referendum in September 1992 by 64% of the electorate. In this way, the NLFA and the Gotthard Tunnel are a material trace of Switzerland's move towards Europe. Thus, the paradox: the same Switzerland that said "no" to Europe contributed to the building of European transport networks and alone bore the roughly CHF 20 billion cost, with no access to European aid. This situation raised controversy between the various Swiss political parties. For some of our respondents, Switzerland's position is not justified while, for others, the fact that it financed the entire project should have allowed the country to maintain autonomy over decisions regarding the infrastructure's management.

The construction of new transport infrastructure across Switzerland must also be seen in the broader context of bilateral negotiations in the land transport sector (the latter being one of the seven bilateral agreements signed between Switzerland and Europe in June 1999). While this question is seemingly simple, the case gave rise to intense debates in Switzerland (Schwok, 2015). Effectively, Europe had been aiming to increase its north-south road transport capacities in light of limits imposed by Switzerland, and notably the ban on traffic for vehicles over 28 tons. At the same time, the Swiss government for its part had been targeting a modal shift policy in favor of rail for freight traffic across the Alps. The bilateral agreement signed in 1999 was a compromise between these two approaches. Switzerland accepted the passage of trucks over 28 tons and, in return, established a performance-related heavy vehicle charge (RPLP) to partially reduce traffic and help finance railway infrastructure. With the implementation of the RPLP, a 40-ton truck pays CHF 325 to travel from Basel to Chiasso. About a quarter of the revenue generated by the RPLP comes from foreign carriers (CHF 4.13 billion between 2002 and 2012) (Département fédéral de l'économie, de la formation et de la recherche, 2015).

The Alps Initiative

Negotiations regarding land transport are not a two-sided debate. Between Europe, which wants to maximize the mobility potential of major cities, and the Swiss government, which is targeting a modal shift strategy from road to rail for Alpine traffic, the Swiss people have taken a clear stance that involves limiting truck transport. Acceptance of the constitutional initiative for the "Protection of Alpine regions against transit traffic" (Alpine Initiative) by 51.9% of voters in February 1994 illustrates this restrictive position.

The initiative was launched by a committee comprised of environmentalists from the Gotthard region with the aim of reducing traffic through the Alps. The constitutional article thus adopted establishes that the traffic of goods through Switzerland on Alpine routes shall be by rail, and that the capacity of the Alpine regions' transit routes are not to be increased. The development of trans-Swiss Alpine transport differs greatly from that of surrounding countries. The transport of goods through the inner Alpine arc (Mont-Cenis/Fréjus in France and Brenner in Austria) represents approximately 100 million tons per year. The breakdown of traffic by country is as follows: 20% through France, 40% through Switzerland and 40% through Austria. This contrasts with the situation in 1980, when traffic was divided in thirds. The rail portion of freight traffic also varies considerably from one country to another: 66.3% in Switzerland, 28% in Austria and only 15% in France (Office fédéral des transports, 2014).

Implementing the Alpine Initiative was not easy, however, and led to tensions between Europe, the Federal Council and the Swiss people. Thus, the initiative has been a topic of debate over the decades. While the Swiss people have shown a clear preference for rail transport on several occasions via different votes, the Initiative des Alpes association recalls that new road sections are to be built by the Confederation and the cantons.

In 2004, a counter-project relative to the "Avanti – for safe and efficient motorways" popular initiative sponsored by the Federal Council and the Parliament was rejected by Swiss voters. This counter-project was designed to complete the national road network and eliminate major bottlenecks. It also provided for the construction of a second Gotthard Tunnel tube based on a modification of the article on the protection of the Alps.

The Second Gotthard Road Tunnel Tube

On February 28, 2016, Swiss voters approved the construction of a second road tunnel tube under the Gotthard with nearly 57% of the vote, but without increasing road capacity (the existing tunnel tube will require regular closing for repairs starting in 2030). The second tunnel tube was designed to bear road traffic during the closure period. The Federal Council maintains that, subsequent to the repair work, only one lane of traffic in either direction will remain open for use. Theoretically, this would comply with the constitutional article on the protection of the Alps. However, it is a controversial topic, and some actors doubt that the plan to leave only one lane open to traffic will actually be respected. The politicians interviewed effectively did not hide the temptation to review the Alpine initiative:

> At the time, we did not oppose the building of trans-Alpine infrastructure. We were in favor of it, and now are also in favor of a second Gotthard tunnel tube for maintenance and security. I won't hide from you the fact that our party would also be favorable to opening it to traffic, but we know that this is legally impossible, so for the time being at least, things are clear. . . . I would say that in general, the Alps initiative cannot be set in stone; it's not because we decided in 1994 that we'll have the same local conditions in 2030 that the agreement is still valid.

The debate on the construction of the second road tunnel tube cannot be completely isolated from the EU's potential desire to maximize use of the existing infrastructure. Federal Transport Councilor Doris Leuthard (2016) at that time stressed this possible pressure from the EU:

> I have a letter from European Transport Commissioner Violeta Bulc that confirms what her predecessor, Siim Kallas, had already guaranteed me in writing. It confirms that our project respects the bilateral agreement on land transport and does not apply capacity restriction. I would like to point out that no one in Brussels has ever questioned me on this subject.

In this same interview, Doris Leuthard highlights another paradoxical element in Swiss transport policy, namely the country's CHF 145 million investment in improving the Gotthard's rail transport capacity in northern Italy:

> The principle of territoriality theoretically prevents investing in infrastructure in a foreign country. But we decided to make an exception. Because it is in the interest of our country to be able to reinforce the transfer freight traffic through the Alps from road to rail. Without this infrastructure in Italy, we'd have to build additional loading terminals in Switzerland.

In addition to assuming infrastructure funding alone, Switzerland in some cases also funds infrastructure abroad. The Gotthard Tunnel is not an isolated case: Switzerland's connection to the European high-speed train network, for example, became a law (law on connection to LGVs, 2005). The country has thus committed to contributing (non-refundable contributions and repayable loans) more than CHF 400 million to fund upgrades in France and Germany. This law aims "to strengthen Switzerland's economic and tourist position and to shift as much international road and air traffic to rail as possible."

Still Via Europaea?

Federal Councilor Willy Ritschard (1979) stated that "our country's history is a page in the history of transport, and our medieval policy of expansion was a transport policy." Our interviewees also seemed aware of the close link between the construction of Switzerland, transport and Europe. While mobility is generally conceived as a destructuring or even destructive force, the country's history shows how control over a particular mobility flow (transit through the Gotthard) became an integrating force. While Switzerland's history indeed cannot be understood without the Gotthard, the latter is incomprehensible without Europe. It was the mobility flows between northern and southern Europe that forced the opening of Schöllenen Gorge.

The relationship between Switzerland, transport and Europe has grown even closer. Switzerland is fighting to maintain control over the mobility flows that cross its territory. The limiting of road transport in favor of rail and the creation of road use charge are its main weapons and also point to its relative autonomy. Guaranteeing their access, however, is a European requirement and a sign of mutual dependence. Solely funding certain infrastructures and contributing to the financing of infrastructures outside its territory is the price Switzerland must pay for being an outsider.

Switzerland, a Country of Highly Mobile Individuals

According to structural census data, more than 10% of working people in Switzerland work 50 kilometers or more from home. Switzerland has become a country of long-distance commuters in just a few years. However, this general observation overshadows key disparities between categories of working people: men and people with high levels of training and high salaries in positions of hierarchical responsibility are largely over-represented among these high commuters. There is also an under-representation of people with children among long-distance commuters.

In the midst of a housing crisis in several major Swiss cities in a country with hourly or half-hourly rail service and relatively affordable transport passes (in terms of buying power), the math is easy. However, its implications in terms of social inequalities, territorial development, lifestyles, identity or social cohesion are frequently ignored.

The Injunction to Reversible Mobility

Beyond the general observation of an entire country that is becoming like a big-city neighborhood in terms of daily life and uses, commuting also reveals inequalities between inhabitants. Contemporary Western societies require specific mobility skills that are increasingly becoming a precondition for socio-professional integration. Being flexible, knowing how land on one's feet, being open to opportunities – so many conditions for a successful life, both professionally and personally. This observation was confirmed in several recent Swiss and European research projects on the subject (Viry & Kaufmann, 2015), as well as in our interviews with different actors:

> if we travel a lot nowadays, it's not because we like to. When both household members work, it's difficult to find work in the same city, so sometimes one of us has to commute. Before, when people worked in the same place for 20 years, you could move to a place, and back then only men worked, so it was easy for the household to manage. Nowadays, it's very complicated because people change jobs every two or three years, and there are two of us changing jobs every two or three years.

This injunction to be mobile and obligation to be flexible geographically and schedule-wise was decreed by the Swiss law on unemployment 20 years ago:

> The unemployment law says you are obliged to accept . . . a job if it's within a two-hour commute from your home.

People are not equal when it comes to being flexible in time and space. Research indicates that there are significant differences within the population, between those who build their lifestyle around being mobile and those who have no aspiration to work-related mobility due to strong local ties. More notably even, it appears that people who have already had mobility experience are often more willing and prepared to be mobile again. On the other hand, those with no mobility experience typically do not express the desire to seize such professional opportunities. This suggests a clear disposition to mobility and a specific relationship to space (uprooting, having several domiciles, etc.), an inclination that is more frequently observed among high income, highly educated people.

In Switzerland, while the ability to be flexible is clearly and in many ways a career "accelerator," it also reveals very marked gender inequalities. While women are just as mobile as men prior to coupledom, the latter widens the gap between the sexes. In fact, "shacking up" is associated with longer commutes for men and shorter commutes for women. Becoming a parent further accentuates this weakening of professional mobility for both women and men. Parenthood in Switzerland is associated with a sharp decline in women's employment, and while some simply choose to work less, others choose to leave the job market entirely. These phenomena are deeply rooted in the country's socio-economic structures (lack of childcare services, greater emphasis on personal responsibilities, etc.). This leads to the prioritizing of the male partner's career, so that it is more often the woman who follows in the event of a professional move and adapts by finding a job closer to home, if she continues to work.

Hence, mobility is an ambivalent factor that is nonetheless instrumental for keeping the family unit together while allowing access to jobs via commuting. In this way, it would seem that reversible mobility is completely changing Swiss family life.

Switzerland by Train and Switzerland by Car

Lurking behind social inequalities are marked spatial disparities. Two Switzerlands – one Train-centric and the other Car-centric – live side by side when it comes to regional development. The former is wealthy and eminently urban while the latter is peripheral. However, "train Switzerland" does not fit in to country's urbanization map. Some cities and towns such as Chaux-de-Fonds are poorly connected by rail, while other outlying regions are well served. Haut-Valais and central Switzerland are two such examples, thanks in large part to the Lötschberg and Gotthard rail tunnels.

The very existence of a "train Switzerland," a sort of large reticular city inhabited by commuters, makes rail operators and their service policies central when it comes to regional planning. And when it comes to regional planning, the devil is in the details. Thus, the Swiss Federal Railways (CFF) changes its routes and stops – sometimes erratically – but above all gives preference to major routes. That is how Nyon, for instance, lost ICN trains service to trains serving Yverdon, Neuchâtel and Bienne in December 2015. Similarly, and due to the same schedule change, Basel is no longer connected to French-speaking Switzerland, as half-hourly service between Geneva and Zurich was opted for instead.

Such policies only reinforce the antagonism between train Switzerland and car Switzerland, especially since trains no longer wait for connections. For some of our respondents, however, this policy is counterproductive because it is divisive and, in some ways, inconsistent.

On February 9, 2014, the Federal Decree Regulating the Financing and Development of Railway Infrastructure (FAIF) was approved by Swiss voters. As promoters of the decree, the Federal Council and Parliament "want[ed] to ensure the rail network's operation, maintain its current operating system and adapt capacities to a growing demand" "given the increase in traffic." As "existing rail infrastructure no longer allows for substantial improvement of the offer," the FAIF has been portrayed as a tool for ensuring "an attractive rail offer," which "is an asset to the country's economy." The February 9, 2014, vote on the FAIF is paradoxical in this respect. On the one hand was the question of investing to promote a shift from road to rail; on the other hand, the de facto desire to invest only concerned the reticular city of train Switzerland (i.e., inter-city and intramuros service in major cities).

Yet, with the recent, large-scale rise in part-time telecommuting (one day a week or a few hours a day to enjoy better travel conditions), the cards may fall differently. Telecommuting increases workers' flexibility in space and time, thereby allowing them to live further away. While telecommuting is not possible in all professions, advantages in terms of flow management are real. Moreover, it appears that telecommuting very well might reduce the divide between car Switzerland and train Switzerland. Fewer commutes means the possibility of expanding employment areas and living even further from the workplace, with fewer or no schedule constraints.

Territorial Integration

A rapid transport offer in Switzerland improved by the implementation of the FAIF rail program, along with an increase in telecommuting is clearly amplifying the reversible mobility trend. Reversible mobility occurs when transport and telecommunication tools are used to minimize the effects of travel on social life.

The increase in reversibility brings us to the heart of the paradoxical challenges of mobility: the more the Swiss commute, the more sedentary they become. Swiss residents are already moving less to other regions of the country. Figures from the Federal Statistical Office highlight this phenomenon: never before has interregional migration been so low in Switzerland, a trend that is likely to intensify in the future. Yet, in such a country, is there not a risk of impoverishment, or even of national cohesion? "There are very few people who cross the language barrier for work. A few in the Bern region and in the Biel area, that's it," one interviewee reported. Is this not dangerous for Switzerland, a country that is a marriage of convenience between cultures, where one must regularly make an intellectual effort to remember why we live in the same country?

This question is quite evidently not on the political agenda. And yet, it is crucial because the reversibility phenomenon carries the seeds of socio-spatial segregation and undoubtedly those of different forms of communitarianism, which are all the more powerful as they can be reinforced by the country's highly decentralized cantonal institutional organization. The often-fragile balance between the urban and rural worlds, linguistic spaces and different faiths was forged by the obligation to get to know one another for linguistic or work-related reasons, or when the transport system was such that workers were obliged to uproot from one canton to go live and work in another. How to replace these vectors of social cohesion if people no longer move?

This question is paradoxical and merits broader political debate. The ambiguity lies in the fact that the current situation exists due to the excellence of Switzerland's rail service, which is central to Swiss identity. Today, the train is an essential part of Swissness but at the same time carries significant risks for national cohesion.

The Swiss Archipelago?

With the development of infrastructure and mobility services, the Swiss territory has undergone considerable changes in recent years. The construction and spread of new infrastructures have effectively improved Switzerland's territorial integration. In other words, the different parts of the country are more easily accessible than in the past.

However, as territorial integration advances, the possibilities with regard to distance are also increasing. Reversible mobility allows individuals to keep a safe distance between the different cultural regions while ensuring exchanges. Swiss citizens can travel anywhere in the country while remaining "at home." The same goes for Swiss families, who are more mobile than ever but can also more readily avoid changing regions definitively thanks to high-speed transport, despite distances.

While Switzerland is preparing to face increased mobility, certain individuals and territories seem increasingly isolated. Speed allows us to travel farther, but the feeling of not having more time is becoming widespread. In this sense, Switzerland is much like an archipelago connected by rapid but often temporary mobilities.

Switzerland's Financial Role

A Pole of Attraction

It is clear that the ability to attract capital flows, companies and economic activities is an important asset for Switzerland. The country's economic openness, in this sense, has often been cited (Weder, 2007). In a world of mobile capital, Switzerland is enjoying the benefits. While most agree with this observation, opinions differ on the "beneficial" nature of this situation. For some interviewees, Switzerland's attractiveness and international flows are an opportunity to strengthen economic growth and endogenous development, provided that reinvestment policies are judicious. For other interviewees, the risks and limitations seem obvious. The latter thus feel an urgent need to "control," "curb" or "limit" certain mobility flows and cite the "negative" effects of an "overheating" of the Swiss economy and its "border industry."

Some of the key "framework conditions" that make Switzerland so attractive have more recently become the subject of controversy. Differences in the tax treatment policies for companies between the different cantons is one example: as the Federal Department of Finance points out, in a context where the taxation of companies faces fierce international tax competition, Switzerland's preferential taxation of the foreign income of certain companies has been criticized by the Organization for Economic Cooperation and Development (OECD) and the EU. Thus, it has been forced to adapt its tax system while attempting to strengthen its attractiveness to businesses and maintain [its] economic competitiveness. It is precisely the ability to keep "mobile activities" in Switzerland that is the focus of the debate. The reform should help eliminate differences in the tax benefit treatment of Swiss and foreign companies within the framework of cantonal taxes. It should also result in an overall reduction in the corporate tax rate, as well as balance Switzerland's attractiveness capacity with the need adapt at the international level.

There is a consensus as regards the need for corporate tax reform, as the pressure on Switzerland has been insurmountable. In fact, there is no other choice. However, this reform raises concerns. While, for some, the reform is an opportunity for a higher average tax contribution from companies, others consider that Switzerland must remain vigilant with regard to economic attraction and competition with other countries. The question of the distribution of economic growth also is raised, insofar as the envisaged reform should standardize canton tax rates. The reform is thus an opportunity to rethink the balance between economic competition, tax contribution and territorial balance.

The same tensions between economic competition, tax fairness and territorial balance emerge around the issue of tax packages. In Switzerland, some foreign nationals have the option of being taxed based on expenditure (lump-sum taxation) and not income and actual assets. This type of tax has helped attract wealthy households to Switzerland: in 2012, 5,634 people (60% from French-speaking Switzerland) were subject to this tax regime. In that same year, these same people paid approximately CHF 700 million to the country's various institutions. Roughly 22,497 jobs are said to be linked to the existence of this type of tax. In November 2014, the "Stop millionaire tax privileges (abolition of tax packages)" popular initiative aimed at "making tax privileges illegal" was voted down. Its initiators felt that Switzerland "[did] not need to attract extremely wealthy, tax-savvy foreigners." Faced with this initiative and aware of the "[keen] international competition to attract wealthy and highly mobile taxpayers," the Federal Council considered that lump-sum taxation increased Switzerland's attractiveness. In January 2010, the canton of Zurich abolished lump-sum taxation following a popular vote. Of the 201 people taxed under this system in the canton, 67 moved to other cantons and 30 left Switzerland before the end of 2010.

The role of capital flows also revealed a paradox as regards Switzerland's economic attractiveness. On January 15, 2015, the Swiss National Bank abolished the floor rate of CHF 1.20 per euro introduced in September 2011. This measure was designed to help in dealing with the veritable rush for the safe haven the Swiss franc represented following the debt crisis in the euro zone. With the end of the floor rate, the value of the Swiss franc soared 30% against the euro in a matter of hours. With the exchange rate, frontier workers gained 16% buying power overnight with the same salary level in Swiss francs.

The "strong franc (franc fort)" thus plays an ambivalent role. Swiss consumers – especially border residents – are favored by higher purchasing power. At the same time, the strengthening of the franc poses a problem as regards competitiveness for Swiss companies vis-à-vis foreign competitors. Certain branches such as manufacturing and tourism are highly susceptible to the risks of a strong franc, while sectors with higher added value such as the pharmaceutical industry are less so.

Based on these different elements, we understand that Swiss finance industry is undergoing changes. In 2012, the financial sector represented 10.3% of the country's added value and employed 5.7% of the country's employees (Association suisse des banquiers, 2012). With the international economic crisis, one of the fundamental pillars of Switzerland's finance industry – banking secrecy – was very much called into question at the international level. Faced with international pressure, Switzerland has been forced to abolish banking secrecy for foreign taxpayers; its future for Swiss citizens is not certain today either.

The changes in the Swiss financial sector were also a topic of discussion during our interviews. While there was general unanimity regarding the need to reorganize the sector, some of our respondents mentioned the risk of loss of competitiveness in this area.

Territorial Permanence, Reticular Permeability?

Switzerland is characterized by an efficient balance of strong territorial roots and stability, as well as its ability to attract and manage flows at the global level. Switzerland's attractiveness therefore results from this double dynamic of territorial permanence and reticular permeability, meaning its ability to appropriate the various flows associated with globalization.

While socio-spatial analyses have traditionally distinguished between the space of places and the space of flows, our analysis shows that the two logics overlap considerably in the Swiss case, and feed into one another. The "framework conditions" our respondents refer to on several occasions are the basis of this territorial stability. A variety of considerations determine these conditions, including quality of life, institutional stability and advantageous fiscal conditions for economic players. This balance is difficult to manage, as reticular flows often disrupt and destabilize the territory, thus threatening quality of life and creating political tensions and outside demands with regard to tax standards.

The slow pace of the Swiss political system and fragmenting and diversity of the institutional framework seem unfavorable conditions for controlling such flows. Likewise, the reticular space seems doomed to expand in urban and metropolitan settings. And yet, it is in this Switzerland of direct democracy, decentralization and

Alpine landscapes that flows arrive, slow down and become territory. Moreover, it is this territorial permanence that, in turn, feeds and renews reticular permeability.

Questioning Immigration

To the south of the Gotthard is the canton of Ticino, which has a population of around 300,000 and whose official language is Italian. Ticino is the only Swiss canton located south of the Alps. It enjoys a mild climate and beautiful landscapes, which make it a privileged tourist destination. The canton is located between two metropolitan systems: the Swiss urban system to the north and the northern Italian system to the south (Sezione dello sviluppo territoriale del Cantone Ticino, 2009). Milan has around six million inhabitants. Until the mid-20th century, the canton's economy depended on the agricultural sector and public sector activities. It was not until the 1950s that Ticino saw a period of industrialization and economic growth. The canton has become one of the country's leaders in the service sector, and Lugano is now its third largest financial center. Nevertheless, over the past three decades, its economic development has been less dynamic than that of the rest of Switzerland. From the 1980s, the mobility of people within the canton and transit traffic have increased considerably with the opening of the first Gotthard road tunnel. The Cantonal Master Plan concludes that Ticino risks becoming an "economic corridor without profit," a "residential satellite of the Lombard metropolitan area," "double periphery for Zurich in the north and Milan in the south" (Sezione dello sviluppo territoriale del Cantone Ticino, 2009, p. 34).

On the occasion of the vote for against mass immigration on February 9, 2014, Ticino inhabitants voted 68% in favor of the initiative – the highest cantonal score for this vote. In all likelihood, this result is directly linked to the Ticinese perception of the arrival of Italian workers in the canton in recent years. A study on the Ticinese job market published in September 2015 (and that was the subject of much controversy) calls to mind the main figures (IRE, 2015): with more than 62,500 people in 2014, the number of people working in Switzerland and living abroad has almost doubled since 2002. As a result, roughly one in four workers in Ticino is a cross-border worker. In a Swiss context of more than 300,000 cross-border workers in 2015 (15,000 in 2000), Ticino is the canton with highest number of cross-border workers after Geneva (80,000) and is ahead of cantons such as Basel-City (35,000) and Vaud (28,000). Switzerland has 165,000 cross-border workers residing in France, 70,000 in Italy, 60,000 in Germany and 8,000 in Austria. Almost all cross-border workers in Ticino reside in Italy.

Border Paradoxes

Cross-border dynamics linked to differences in prices and salaries on either side of the border create paradoxical situations. It is worth noting that the end of the floor tax rate offered cross-border workers a proportional increase in their wages. As such, some Swiss citizens fear an increase in unemployment and wage dumping due to the pressure exerted by cross-border workers. However, the Institute for Economic Research study (IRE, 2015) recalls that Ticino has reported solid economic growth and employment in the 12 years since the introduction of the free movement of persons and considers that this growth has notably been driven by foreign workers and cross-border workers in particular. While concluding that cross-border employment would not have increased the risk of unemployment for the local population, the study recognizes that the abundant supply of foreign workers in the labor market creates fierce competition, and that it is conceivable that the root of the problem does not so much lie in risk of unemployment as in access to the labor market.

The border issue in general and situation in Ticino more specifically were recurring themes during discussions with our respondents. Cross-border workers are generally considered an economic necessity for Switzerland, but all parties seem to agree that this immigration is poorly managed, especially in certain cantons like Ticino. Our respondents proposed a variety of "accompanying measures" to limit the undesirable effects of border dynamics. In some cases, these measures would aim to control the labor market as well as introduce new ways of taxing cross-border workers; in others, they would also strive to improve accessibility conditions in terms of transport.

With regard to these "accompanying measures," some respondents were in favor of implementing policies aimed at training and valorizing native workers. According to some of our interviewees, the opportunity – priority even – must be given to Swiss workers:

> At some point we still have to be careful because we have to ask ourselves: does our market offer the people who live here the chance to find a place in [it]? Or do we prefer to say forget it because it requires high levels of training and then simply go look for these people on the other side of the border? Shouldn't we take more coherent and stronger measures so that we can put our own people who have the profiles we're looking for on the labor market?

Others, on the contrary, consider that the solution lies in policy limiting tax competition between the two sides of the border.

Social Pressure

While border dynamics seem to partially explain the February 9, 2014, vote result, changes in migration flows further elucidate this question. With the onset of the economic crisis in the late 2000s, the net migration rate of foreigners to Switzerland has grown significantly, soaring to over 100,000 people in 2008 and dropping to around 80,000 in 2014. In this year, almost three-quarters of new arrivals in Switzerland came from EU countries, namely Germany (about 25,000 people), Italy (19,000), Portugal (15,000) and France (14,000).

With "population growth" as a consequence of "uncontrolled immigration," the promoters of the initiative "against mass immigration" pleaded for "autonomous" regulation and control of migratory flows to Switzerland. To act on "the consequences of this disastrous development," its defenders proposed targeting the mobility projects of foreign populations by limiting their entry. Thus, the solution was not so much to act on the possible issues associated with this mobility as to limit mobility itself.

Switzerland is no stranger to managing immigration flows. In 2014, the Federal Statistical Office counted nearly two million descendants of first-generation immigrant parents (including 1.4 million foreigners born abroad and 540,000 naturalized people born abroad). Regarding second-generation migration, there were 480,000 immigrant-born residents in Switzerland (50% of whom have been naturalized and 40% of whom have at least one parent born abroad). Between 2003 and 2014, the non-immigrant population fell from 70% to 64%.

Our respondents' views on immigration diverged. Like border flows, immigration was seen as an opportunity and a necessity, but also as a threat and a burden. Yet, isolationist positions did not emerge in our interviews. On the contrary, all seemed to agree that migratory dynamics are a part of contemporary societies.

Our respondents explained the result of the February 9, 2014, vote in two ways. Immigration is seen as a threat to the labor market, as the arrival of newcomers contributed to the lowering of wages and increased unemployment, as well as a burden benefitting from social assistance. The figure of the immigrant – at once, a job stealer and a freeloader – paradoxically is doubly threatening.

Territorial Pressure

It is around the notion of *Dichtestress* – or "stress linked to density" – that another type of argument was developed by the founders of the initiative. According to this idea, demographic growth as a result of migratory flows exerts pressure on the territory, infrastructure and housing. Newcomers would thus be the culprits of this development.

Moreover, on November 30, 2014, a few months after the approval of the initiative against mass immigration, the Swiss rejected the ECOPOP initiative (Stop overpopulation – Yes to the sustainable preservation of natural resources), which targeted environmental pollution. Unlike the mass immigration initiative, it was in this case the issue of population growth more specifically that was the object of regulation. Attention initially focused more on managing the stock (i.e., population) than on managing flows (migration). More specifically, the initiative considered that population growth must be "compatible with the sustainable preservation of natural resources." The promoters of the initiative insisted that limiting population growth is essential for the sustainable management of resources.

However, the first way of acting on stock management is by controlling immigration. In paragraph 2 of the proposed new article, the initiative establishes that "the increase in Switzerland's permanent resident population resulting from net migration cannot exceed 0.2% per year on an average of three years." Thus, unlike the initiative against mass immigration, the ECOPOP (CFS, 2014) initiative specifically aimed to define the limits of migratory flows:

> The Mass Immigration Initiative requires quotas but does not set limits. That's the Federal Council's job, but [it] wants immigration all the way. The mass immigration initiative is therefore insufficient, so the people must set clear limits.

The argument advanced in the case of the ECOPOP initiative was therefore environmental. Switzerland is presented as an ecosystem comprised of a population and natural resources whose balance must be respected. In this new approach, it is no longer the figure of the immigrant, foreigner or cross-border worker that is used to justify the initiative, but rather that of metropolization. For defenders of the ECOPOP, the threat is clear: "Switzerland will become a megalopolis" (CFS, 2014). It is therefore the desire to "stop concrete" (ECOPOP, 2014) that is the driving force for action: "I don't want a city that stretches from Lake Geneva to Lake Constance! Let's stop concreting Switzerland" (Meier, 2014). Concreting is synonymous with urbanization and an increase in buildable areas. Densification will ultimately only delay complete concrete coverage. Indeed, according to the initiative's supporters, higher population densities lead to an increase in the consumption of natural resources. Increased mobility, for instance, is therefore considered a direct effect of population growth. However, density-related stress was a dubious argument to the minds of some respondents, who considered immigration flows and densification as separate and distinctive processes. Indeed, it was mainly in areas of higher density stress (e.g., metropolitan areas) that opposition to the "initiative on mass immigration" was the greatest.

More than a Neighborhood Problem

If the result of the vote of February 9, 2014, caused a scandal, it is because the choice of the Swiss inhabitants affected all European citizens. While surveys at the European level demystify a possible Swiss xenophobia (Koch & Lavenex, 2007), the Swiss decision raised a series of antipathies. Given this, analysing the choice of the Swiss is as important as observing its neighbors' reactions. It is important to recall that the reaction to the result of the Swiss vote was not unanimous; European public opinion was disturbed by its outcome. European press reviews evoked "withdrawal," "isolation," "an island," "confinement," "rupture," "challenge," "identity vote," "fear" and "obstacles." In general, the press considered the result bad news, and certain European leaders encouraged European institutions and representatives to react. However, it also seemed to generally agree that the vote was not only (and not mainly) a Swiss problem.[1] While the result of the 1992 referendum to join the European Economic Area (EEA) could be considered a problem between Europe and Switzerland at the time, the February 9, 2014, vote above all exposed the problem of Europe. While alluding to the possible negative economic consequences for Switzerland, the European press notably wondered about its consequences for Europe. Concerns about a possible tsunami effect with Switzerland as the epicenter, or a contagion effect, grew. The French newspaper *Libération* (11/02/2014) spoke of the "Swiss virus" in reference to the French political context.

Not all of Europe mourned the result of the vote. Some groups welcomed the Swiss decision, like France's then National Front president Jean-Marie Le Pen who, wondering if "the EU would send in its tanks," affirmed that the French would also have voted the same way if such a referendum were launched in that country.[2] In the U.K., the leader of the Independence Party (UKIP) regarded the Swiss result as "wonderful news for lovers of freedom and national sovereignty in Europe."[3] The spokesperson for the Alternative for Germany (AfD), Bernd Lucke,[4] and the founder of the Netherlands' Freedom Party (PVV), Geert Wilders,[5] considered Switzerland's choice an example for immigration control. Similar comments were made by representatives of the Austrian Freedom Party and the Norwegian Progress Party.

These groups' reactions echo their own proposals with regard to immigration policies. The Swiss decision therefore fuels positions calling for more restrictive regulation of migratory flows. The problem with this position is that it is also the very members of these political parties that the initiative targeted. The celebration of this vote by these foreign groups is therefore paradoxical insofar as the initiative also limits the mobility potential of French, English, German, Dutch, Austrian and Norwegian citizens, among others, towards Switzerland.

Italy's Northern League's position was disconcerting to say the least. This party, which calls for the creation of a macro-region in northern Italy independent from the rest of the country, has traditionally favored restrictive immigration policies. The federal secretary of the party, Matteo Salvini, thus welcomed the Swiss decision, which notably aimed "to give jobs to the Swiss first."[6]

European institutions, however, quickly expressed their dismay at the Swiss vote. The European Commission voiced this most clearly, saying that the initiative for the introduction of immigration quotas had been passed through this vote.[7]

European Commission President at that time José Manuel Barroso declared that the Swiss vote posed "serious problems," "especially for Switzerland," and warned that the free movement of people "is an essential element" and "cannot be negotiated."[8] European Commissioner for Employment, Social Affairs and Inclusion László Andor similarly told the European Parliament that "quotas are contrary to the principle of free movement," and that this principle was not only an essential part of the internal market but was the very heart of relations with Switzerland.[9]

While the European Commissioner insists that this decision should not be seen as a "punishment" or "sanction" in reaction to the choice of Swiss voters,[10] his response proves European institutions' determination in facing the challenges surrounding the integration project. The reaction was addressed more specifically to those who, in one way or another, had a mind to challenge the future of Europe and the legitimacy of European institutions in the May 2014 European Parliament elections. As ex-EU negotiator David O'Sullivan said in October 2014, you just have to understand that votes also have consequences.[11]

Part of the debate around the "against mass immigration" initiative also has to do with the consequences of questioning the principle of free movement. As this principle is one of the fundamental bilateral agreements between Switzerland and the EU, its rupture calls other agreements into question, due to the existence of a "guillotine clause." Let us recall that the ratification of the agreement on free movement and its extensions to new Member States resulted in "very emotional" referendums (Schwok, 2015, p. 34).

Scandalous Ambiguity

The Swiss vote indeed caused a scandal; some of its European neighbors perceived it as an affront while others welcomed it as a revolutionary move. It was, in any event, characterized by a basic ambiguity: while the title "against mass immigration" expresses a certain radicalism, its acceptance opens a period of decision and incremental negotiation.

This ambiguity is the result of the initiative's dual meaning. It carries a nationalist message: the Swiss initiative explicitly aimed to regain decision-making power over questions of immigration. The new constitutional article thus establishes that "Switzerland autonomously manages the immigration of foreigners."[12] Moreover, the initiators of the initiative unabashedly call to defend the country's independence: "Get involved so that Switzerland can maintain its independence" (CFS, 2014).

However, it would be misleading to view the Swiss initiative as a simple claim for pure ancestral sovereignty. While its initiators call for "territorial sovereignty" of the "valleys," it is nonetheless part of a new logic of power that emphasizes flow management. The initiative opens the door to a "marketisation" (Favell & Hansen, 2002) of immigration wherein decisions will be taken "according to the overall economic interests of Switzerland" (art. 121a, paragraph 3).

The initiative indeed introduces a fundamental distinction between "legislation on foreigners and asylum" (art. 121) and "immigration management" (art. 121a). The first involves prohibiting, authorizing or regulating "entry into," "exit from," and "stays" and the "establishment of foreigners in" Switzerland. The legislation defines the citizenship status of non-nationals (rights and obligations), thus targeting foreigners. When it comes to "managing" immigration, however, its focus is on flows. The management of such as "ceilings" and "quotas" is based more on economic calculations than on legal principles.

Hence, the initiative combines autonomy in theory (the Swiss decide . . .) and delegation in practice (. . . depending on the Swiss economy). This second meaning creates a paradox vis-à-vis the initiative: if "Switzerland's overall economic interests" so require, immigration could very well increase beyond the very levels the initiative seems to want to limit. Most likely aware of this paradox, its initiators insist that "managing and controlling immigration also inevitably means limiting it"(Comité interpartis, 2013, p. 6).

The popular initiative, which was presented as an assertion of national sovereignty, thus highlights the preponderance of economic considerations over all others. Questions of demography, sustainable development and cultural identity thus become background issues. While the initiative's founders often cite negative effects such as population explosion, the increase in resource and energy consumption, and pressure on transport infrastructure and the housing market, they dissociate these phenomena from the initiative's primary aim, which is to make "the overall economic interests of Switzerland" "predominant" (Comité interpartis, 2013, p. 6).

The initiative seeks to address neither the consequences of immigration, nor its causes. As its proponents admit, "immigration is driven by a healthy economy" (Comité interpartis, 2013, p. 7) and is basically a laissez-faire (non-) policy. Formulated as such, the syllogism leaves little doubt: if immigration is the result of the host country's economic situation and decisions concerning its management are based on economic need, immigration flows will continue as long as the economic situation is favorable. UDC vice-president Christoph Blocher bluntly affirmed this viewpoint when he stated that "economically-useful foreigners can come, others cannot."[13]

It would indeed seem that the essential question is not *how many* but *who*: who has the right to come to Switzerland? In other words, it is not so much a question of numbers as of quality. Our respondents effectively recognized that the issue does not lie in specifying figures.

The initiative effectively makes a choice on "principle" by establishing that "ceilings" and "quotas" must also be set "in accordance with the principle of national preference" (CFS, 2014), which can influence the volume of migratory flows.

Another principle of "European non-preference" was established simultaneously. As the initiative's founders point out, the proposed regulations make it possible to not differentiate between "European foreigners" and those "from other regions of the world" (Comité interpartis, 2013, p. 6).

Qualitatively speaking, while these new "principles" introduce significant changes in how immigration is handled, decisions about flow volumes seem to be determined by a demand for mobility driven by economic dynamics. In this respect, what seemed like an initiative to "take control" of immigration policy in reality appears to be dependent on the laws of the market.

Will the Market Provide?

All of our respondents recognized that part of the Swiss population has come under pressure due to the increase in migratory flows. Identity and even security arguments alone do not seem to explain the acceptance of this initiative. On the contrary, the problems of wage dumping, unemployment risk and difficulties entering the labor market are most likely the main reasons behind the adoption of this decision. While the argument of the societal burden of immigrants may have played a role, it is secondary to the aforementioned ones. Likewise, pressure on certain facilities, especially housing, has accentuated the sense of pressure on the territory. The February 2014 vote was indeed a reflection of a certain unease whose underlying causes are real.

Yet, is the new constitutional article the right answer to this unease? Is the very principle of free movement at its origin? In trying to understand the wording of the constitutional article, we have attempted to highlight its ambiguity from a mobility standpoint. While the article was presented as a way of limiting immigration, it appears to be much less restrictive in its implementation. In our opinion, the fundamental aim of the new article has to with the need to meet Switzerland's economic interests, in which case elements such as culture, territory and quality of life are second-level priorities when it comes to managing migratory flows. While the principle of national preference helps in explaining this interpretation, it may prove difficult to implement in practice. If the priority is to defend "Switzerland's overall economic interests," national preference may also remain a secondary principle.

The vote also shed light on a paradox in Switzerland's direct democracy system. Effectively, it is not only the results of the vote that pose a problem; it is also the very principle of popular voting. Direct democracy as practiced in Switzerland – and which is one of the great specificities of the Swiss political system – in many respects seems difficult to reconcile with the methodology and procedures applied in the European integration process. Some observers have already noted that the "great Swiss weakness" with regard to the European project "is that the government cannot guarantee that an agreement signed at the international level will actually come into force" insomuch as "the constant threat of opponents of the Federal Council to resort to a referendum if [the agreement] makes too many concessions" is omnipresent (Schwok, 2015, p. 25). While it is true that European leaders are careful not to explicitly question the specific nature of the Swiss political tradition, the revoking of agreements between Europe and Switzerland through direct participation procedures is a constant threat in the eyes of European partners.

Conclusion

This chapter explored the debates on the different forms of mobility in Switzerland by considering the political debates surrounding a series of popular votes. What can we conclude from this analysis of the Swiss case? One essential point is that the deep political divides around the different types of mobility reconstruct certain constitutive rifts within Swiss society, and in particular the debate on the role of the market, separation of church and State and the center-periphery dichotomy. These conflicts have not disappeared but have become less marked, and their ability to take into account social and societal changes has become quite fragmented. It is only by describing the relationship to the different forms of mobility discussed in this chapter that it is now possible to draft an overall sketch of the major political conflicts at work. The personal, lived experience of mobility coupled with media hype and collective rhetoric on the subject feed our relationship with the world and with others, and transform the political balance.

Notes

1. https://www.bilan.ch/economie/immigration_la_presse_s_interroge_sur_les_consequences_du_vote; https://www.rts.ch/info/suisse/5599651-la-presse-etrangere-sinterroge-sur-limpact-du-vote-antiimmigration.html; https://www.letemps.ch/suisse/suisse-ferme-frontieres-va-confrontation-bruxelles.
2. https://www.lepoint.fr/politique/immigration-le-pen-appelle-les-francais-a-suivre-l-exemple-suisse-10-02-2014-1790313_20.php
3. https://www.lepoint.fr/monde/referendum-suisse-l-ue-s-inquiete-l-extreme-droite-se-rejouit-10-02-2014-1789893_24.php
4. https://www.ft.com/content/226ea1a8-9339-11e3-8ea7-00144feab7de
5. https://www.ft.com/content/df9c32f4-94c9-11e3-9146-00144feab7de
6. https://www.quotidiano.net/esteri/2014/02/10/1023603-immigrazione-svizzera-referendum-ue.shtml
7. https://ec.europa.eu/commission/presscorner/detail/fr/MEMO_14_96
8. https://ec.europa.eu/commission/presscorner/detail/fr/STATEMENT_14_7
9. https://ec.europa.eu/commission/presscorner/detail/en/STATEMENT_14_32
10. https://ec.europa.eu/commission/presscorner/detail/en/STATEMENT_14_32
11. Interview with David O'Sullivan (05min54s) https://www.rts.ch/info/suisse/6261764-les-negociations-suisseue-sont-dans-limpasse-selon-david-osullivan.html
12. https://www.bk.admin.ch/ch/f/pore/vi/vis413t.html
13. http://www.tdg.ch/suisse/christoph-blocher-s-prend-citadins/story/19621715

References

Association suisse des banquiers. (2012). *L'importance de la place financière suisse*. Bâle: Association suisse des banquiers.

Bovy, P. H. (1989). La Suisse et le développement du réseau ferroviaire européen à haute performance. *Ingénieurs et Architectes Suisses*, 33–45.

CFS. (2014). *Votation populaire du 30 novembre 2014. Explications du Conseil fédéral*. Conseil Fédéral Suisse. Retrieved January 15, 2021, from https://www.bk.admin.ch/dam/bk/fr/dokumente/Abstimmungsbuechlein/explications_du_conseilfederal.pdf.download.pdf/explications_du_conseilfederal09022014.pdf

Comité interpartis. (2013). *Argumentaire Initiative populaire "contre l'immigration de masse"*. Comité interpartis contre l'immigration de masse. Retrieved January 15, 2021, from https://www.parlament.ch/centers/documents/fr/argumentarien-pro-f.pdf

Département fédéral de l'économie, de la formation et de la recherche. (2015). *Principes pour une nouvelle politique de croissance*. Retrieved January 15, 2021, from https://www.seco.admin.ch/dam/seco/fr/dokumente/Publikationen_Dienstleistungen/Publikationen_Formulare/Wirtschaftslage/Strukturwandel_Wachstum/Wachstum/Bericht_Neue_Wachstumspolitik_Veroeffentlichung_II_web_.pdf.download.pdf/Rapport_nouvelle_politique_de_croissance_publication_II_web_.pdf

ECOPOP. (2014). *Halte à la surpopulation. Oui à plus de qualité de vie*. Journal de votation pour l'initiative ECOPOP du 30 novembre 2014. Retrieved January 15, 2021, from https://docplayer.fr/66681005-Ecopop-halte-au-betonnage-de-la-suisse-halte-a-la-surpopulation-oui-a-plus-de-qualite-de-vie-ecopop-ja-ch.html

Favell, A., & Hansen, R. (2002). Markets against politics: Migration, EU enlargement and the idea of Europe. *Journal of Ethnic and Migration Studies*, *28*, 581–601.

IRE. (2015). *Approfondimento della situazione del mercato del lavoro ticinese negli anni successivi all'introduzione dell'Accordo sulla Libera Circolazione delle Persone*. IRE- Istituto di Ricerche Economiche, Università della Svizzera italiana. Retrieved January 15, 2021, from https://www.rsi.ch/news/ticino-e-grigioni-e-insubria/Scarica-lo-studio-integrale-in-pdf-6284278.html/binary/Scarica%20lo%20studio%20integrale%20%28in%20pdf%29

Koch, P., & Lavenex, S. (2007). The (contentious) human face of Europeanization: Free movement and immigration. In C. H. Church (Ed.), *Switzerland and the European union: A close, contradictory and misunderstood relationship* (pp. 148–165). New York: Routledge.

Leuthard, D. (January 15, 2016). Le tunnel ferroviaire du Gothard servira d'étalon pour d'autres projets dans le monde. *LeTemps*.

Meier, H. (2014). *Halte à la surpopulation. Oui à plus qualité de vie* (ECOPOP, Ed.). Journal de votation pour l'initiative ECOPOP du 30 novembre 2014.

Miéville, D. S. (2013). *6 décembre 1992, le non de la Suisse à l'Europe*. Lausanne (Suisse): Presses polytechniques et universitaires romandes.

Office fédéral des transports. (2014). *Freight traffic by road and rail through the Swiss Alps 2014*. Retrieved January 15, 2021, from https://www.bav.admin.ch/dam/bav/fr/dokumente/themen/verlagerung/alpenquerender_gueterverkehr2014.pdf.download.pdf/trafic_marchandisesatraverslesalpesen2014.pdf

Ritschard, W. (1979). Préface. In A. Wyss-Niederer (Ed.), *Le saint-gothard via helvetica*. Lausanne: Ovaphil.

Schwok, R. (2015). *Suisse – Union européenne: L'adhésion impossible?* Lausanne: Presses Polytechniques et Univ. Romandes.

Sezione dello sviluppo territoriale del Cantone Ticino. (2009). *Revisione del Piano direttore cantonale Rapporto esplicativo 2009*. Consiglio di Stato della Repubblica e Cantone Ticino. Retrieved January 15, 2021, from https://m4.ti.ch/fileadmin/DT/temi/piano_direttore/rapporto_esplicativo/01_Il_Piano_direttore.pdf

Viry, G., & Kaufmann, V. (Eds.). (2015). *High mobility in Europe: Work and personal life*. Houndmills, Basingstoke Hampshire: Palgrave Macmillan.

Weder, R. (2007). Swiss international economic relations: Assessing a small and open economy. In C. H. Church (Ed.), *Switzerland and the European Union: A close, contradictory and misunderstood relationship* (pp. 99–125). New York: Routledge.

Wyss-Niederer, A. (1979). *Le saint-gothard via helvetica*. Lausanne: Ovaphil.

8

RESONANT MOBILITY FOR DISPLACED PEOPLE

Introduction

Is there any possible Europe beyond mobility? The answer is that mobility will most likely remain a critical element of any ambitious political integration and/or cooperation project in Europe. However, the simplistic and frequently overly optimistic approach taken as regards mobility and that has been applied thus far seemingly cannot neutralize and overcome nationalistic reactions, such as the Brexit. Such reactions can ultimately lead to the abandoning of integration projects. Multiple contradictions have arisen in the last decades. The environmental and social consequences of long-distance mobility are increasingly evident, and an integration model of generalized and intensive mobility is questioned head on. Mobility and immigration flows more specifically have been presented as a mechanism for economic regulation. However, these movements seem to be part of the increasing divide between economically advanced central regions and the periphery of Europe. Also, the supposedly free movement of people across Europe is in flagrant contradiction with restrictions and surveillance of the mobility of non-European populations.

In this view, the real question is not mobility yes or no, but what type of mobility can help forge social and environmental cohesion and political integration across the continent? To review the freedom of movement and residence of persons within Europe, and drawing on Hartmut Rosa (2019), we propose in this conclusion the concept of "resonant mobility" and apply it as a concretization of the principle of free movement.

The analysis we conducted in the preceding pages led us to consider that the way in which mobility has been conceptualized and put into practice in Europe over the last decades has been largely dependent on the neoliberal globalization process and its socio-environmental crises. Mobility has thus been fundamentally

DOI: 10.4324/9780429325014-8

experienced as an end in itself, a tool for crossing the territory, a means of escaping rapidly and frequently. This experience of mobility was largely negative due to its fundamental origin relative to situations of pain, crisis, unemployment and war. With the concept of "resonant mobility," we highlight the contribution that mobility can make not as a way of moving in a territory (in this case Europe), but rather of improving the conditions of encountering and maintaining relationships with other peoples and places.

A Critique of Mobility

We began this book by miniaturizing the European continent and comparing it to a major city. Our goal was to show how a narrative largely founded on the development of mobility had pushed this "continental metropolis" that is Europe into a stalemate from which it has not yet emerged. Like big cities, the bottom-line question posed to inhabitants on a daily basis is whether Europe's inclusive powers are sufficiently strong to ensure the existence of a community of destiny, or if living close together in this space is merely a coincidence. The answer to these questions will undoubtedly depend on political will and future decisions.

Our analysis sought to trace the link between the European integration process and the promotion of different mobility flows. It showed that the integration process has now radically shifted towards a political narrative wherein mobility is unconditionally and systematically encouraged. Freedom of movement had two major goals: firstly, to contribute decisively to the continent's territorial and political integration by strengthening the links between European countries (as a high level of transnational mobility is necessary to increase exchanges, improve mutual knowledge and strengthen the continent's functional integration); secondly, to enable the development of the individual capacities of its inhabitants (workers, students, unemployed, etc.) and ensure their social and professional integration. It is for this reason that job- and training-related mobility, such as the Erasmus program, posted work and frontier work, have been widely encouraged.

But are these statements true? In order to analyze them, we had to develop a conceptual apparatus for understanding mobility (which was the subject of Chapter 2). Thus, we adopted a broad definition of mobility that was inspired by sociology and goes beyond the mere question of movement in geographical space. We defined mobility as the intention and subsequent realization of movement in geographical space that is in one way or another associated with self-transformation of the actors or objects concerned. This definition is advantageous in that it allows us to approach mobility as a socio-spatial phenomenon, an analytical indicator and a social norm. These three facets of the concept of mobility were discussed in Chapter 2 and led to the discovery of a number of ideological tensions based on two contradictory standpoints: that of considering the mobility of people, goods and capital as a priority response to societal problems, or mainly as a source of problems contributing to the concretising of tensions. In the first case, mobility seems synonymous with freedom and is conceived as a creative force, while in the second case it is perceived as a threat and a destabilising force. This fundamental contradiction as such reflects the dichotomy between reversible mobilities (roundtrips made within a short timeframe) and irreversible mobilities (trips not involving an immediate return). Should we promote the cosmopolitanism of exchanges through rapid, frequent, long-distance mobility, or should we promote exchanges through irreversible mobility, which requires strong integration within the host society?

It is from this dichotomy that the ideological divisions that shake up classic political partisan divisions (e.g., left-right opposition, the opposition between statism and anti-statism or even nationalism versus internationalism) are built. When applied to the movement of people, goods or capital, it would appear that ideal types of reversible and irreversible mobility often give rise to hybrid positions. At the two extremes, one naturally identifies two opposing positions: on the one hand, those who favor the mobility (reversible and irreversible) of people, goods and capital, who we termed ultra-liberal, and on the other hand, those who argue for planting roots, living locally and oppose any form of mobility, who we called isolationists. Between these two extremes, four intermediate positions emerged: a *liberal* position that defends reversible tangible and intangible mobility while placing limits on the irreversible mobility of people; a *selective* position as regards the defense of material and immaterial mobility; a *regulatory* position that is generally favorable to the mobility of people but aims to apply certain limits to that of objects and capital and to introduce accompanying measures to regulate migratory flows; and a *localist* position characterized by the defense of local lifestyles.

Through these different positions, one can clearly observe the tension between reversible mobility as it has imposed itself in contemporary societies and much more nuanced ideological positions regarding the supposed benefits of these mobility flows.

Going further, in Chapter 3 we identified a series of interventions explicitly aimed at promoting the different types of mobility implemented at the European level. Throughout its history, the EU has designed and implemented political measures to promote the transnational mobility of different flows. We have distinguished three such types of measures: (de)regulation policies designed to create a common framework as regards the technical and legal conditions of mobility; investment and facility policies aimed at providing the European territory with new infrastructures and territorial capacities; and incentive policies that provide the necessary resources for developing mobility skills and supporting the mobility strategies of individual and collective actors. Although the results of these three types of policies are questionable, they nonetheless represent a coherent, long-term strategy designed to maximize mobility within the EU.

From an individual standpoint, it is obvious that promoting mobility this way has allowed European citizens to partake in the larger transnational mobility project by taking advantage of opportunities in other countries. However, these new opportunities have become norms, turning mobility from a symbol of freedom into a requirement for finding work.

The promotion of mobility through the various policy instruments mentioned above has led to a sharp increase in transport flows across the continent. In addition to the fact that the carbon footprint of these lifestyles is extremely high, it should also be noted that, as they have developed, reversible mobility has become a social norm. The reversal is spectacular: whereas moving fast, far and often was a privileged expression of freedom, these intensive, reversible mobilities are now experienced by many as an obligation to which the employee must submit, a constraining social norm. This observation goes even further, because submission to this norm is accompanied by an increase in inequalities between socio-professional categories, gender inequalities and inequalities between countries and regions according to their airport, rail and motorway accessibility. In this context, motility has become an essential resource for meeting the obligation of mobility in the work world and reconciling professional and private life.

Between countries and regions, the policy of promoting mobility in Europe has also reinforced inequalities. This strategy presents risks from the standpoint of the balance between States, as certain territories tend to enjoy the lion's share of opportunities and become poles of attraction while others see these same opportunities disappear. This observation led us to conclude that the economic growth model associated with a widespread mobility strategy is no longer relevant for Europe and, moreover, generates political opposition from certain actors, who argue in favor of a return of borders or even an exit from the European Union. Brexit-type approaches and the undermining of the EU's foundations can have devastating effects without creating new horizons for the continent. It is clear to us that in the future, integration policies will have to be more sensitive to the undesirable effects of this freedom of movement as it has been exercized in recent decades.

The same can be said for cross-border regions, which are extremely interesting laboratories for observing the dynamics and tensions at play within Europe. Effectively, these regions are historically marked by national borders which, through the interplay of economic differentials, act as a resource for territories and local populations. However, these same regions can become relegated borders, although European integration policies have greatly enhanced them with proactive local and regional cross-border integration policies, notably through development tools and transportation planning. The projects born of this policy are receiving criticism as regards the actual impact on cross-border territories and their inhabitants. While standardized cross-border cooperation mechanisms (INTERREG, EGTC, etc.) help to forge economic and institutional links between cross-border territories, they often neglect the social dimension.

The social dimension of cross-border relations refers to the overlapping of identities, national affiliations, territorial attachment and relationships to otherness in general that form the crux of cross-border social cohesion. However, it also creates disputes between cross-border territories and populations. This type of dissent goes beyond the traditional categories of cross-border integration and calls for new approaches to better grasp the modalities of social cohesion in these regions. In order to go further, we must work to better understand cross-border relationships by analysing experiences of time spent on either side of the border, daily experiences of border crossing and even different forms of attachment and belonging within cross-border territories. Such an approach to the integration and cohesion of cross-border regions would be instrumental in leveraging European public policies by taking into account the lifestyles and identities of inhabitants of these areas.

These different analyses allowed us to conclude that strategies and interventions designed to promote mobility in Europe have seemingly been excessive. Therefore, can we consider that, under certain conditions, opposing mobility may be a legitimate, even reasonable option? What are the arguments against mobility? What forms of mobility are we opposed to? Are there commonalities among the different forms of opposition? In attempting to answer these questions, we have identified the areas in which anti-mobility rhetoric, as we have defined it, are structured. We therefore explored opposition to the construction of major transport infrastructures, anti-immigration rhetoric, anti-mass tourism movements and health-related biosecurity arguments. While the areas and moral justification of the arguments used vary greatly from case to case, we found similarities in the forms of opposition to mobility, the main one being the fact that mobility is generally perceived as a risk for the populations or territories concerned by a given flow. The nature of the risk can vary: social, environmental, economic or, as the COVID-19 pandemic has demonstrated, even existential. These risks have been largely ignored in recent decades. Yet, it was during this period that the European integration process materialized. In fact, the risks associated with mobility flows have been little considered, and measures to deal with and regulate them have at times required a certain degree of improvization in emergency situations. Having politically denied the undesirable effects of and need to find support and control for various flows has sometimes led to a radical critique of the promotion of mobility.

The dovetailing of the different arguments against mobility and sharing of a common argument has become apparent in several concrete cases. These situations, wherein opposition to one type of mobility is based on opposition to another, are generally hybrid. For example, we have seen how the environmental argument paired with opposition to large transportation infrastructure is now being used to contest the increase in immigration flows. We observed the existence of a pro-environment/anti-immigration vision that nuances the identity-based nature of this type of argument. Another example of a hybrid issue is opposition to infrastructure and facilities that promote "overtourism" dynamics, wherein the physical and material infrastructure that ensures accessibility for tourist flows is disputed in order to limit the arrival of tourists. These examples show how difficult it is to dissociate different mobility flows politically. It is therefore natural to develop opposition arguments that take into account their multiplicity.

In order to respond to the promotion of mobility and opposition to this promotion that have developed in different domains, we must take into account its adverse effects and excesses. This will help in highlight the risks and longer-term consequences of mobility-related policies. For example, we can no longer dissociate the investments made in heavy infrastructure from the increase in certain flows or deny that the growth of certain flows automatically leads to a greater demand for infrastructure. Yet, such coherence implies moving away from ultra-liberal/isolationist ideological positions so as to recognize the benefits and issues associated mobility dynamics.

Models of Mobility

The fundamental observation this book makes is that, over the last decades, the process of European integration has been conceived as a unilateral program to promote and increase mobility. Mobility was developed to help eradicate old roots – that implicitly were considered residual – to promote functional integration and possibly, when the time came, to consolidate the "European scale" as a new scale of belonging.

The four freedoms of movement have often been exercized painfully, through competition between territories, economic players and individuals. It is the market that has served as a unifying element, and national systems of protection and rooting have acted as the guardians of diversity and difference. So far, the EU has seemed unable or not yet willing to act as a guarantor not only of mobility but also of integration. The question that arises, therefore, is simple: insofar as European integration as a program for the spread of mobility seems to have reached its limits, can we envisage an alternative?

Comparing Europe and the United States can be instructive in this regard. The "flat world" of the United States (Favell, 2008) has often served as the more or less conscious inspirational model for the construction of Europe. The ideas of freedom, mobility and individualism are indeed closely linked to the American imaginary and seem to have inspired the principle of free movement in Europe. Some observers note that inter-state mobility in the United States is six times greater than migration between EU member countries (although the latter has grown significantly over the past 25 years (Recchi, 2015)), and thus insist that the two realities are not comparable: the United States is a federal state and a nation with a predominant language. However, if, as we have proposed, mobility is to be considered the crossing of space associated with social change (Kaufmann, 2014), then we can conclude that mobility is more intense in Europe than in the U.S. Mobility between European countries implies a capacity for adaptation, flexibility and relationships to otherness that are much more intense than between the constituent states of the United States. In Europe, such change implies changing health systems, education systems, job markets, languages and even lifestyles.

But this questioning goes further because it is not just the fact that the two realities are different: the fundamental question is whether we want them to stay that way. Does the development of Europe mean a partial loss of heritage for its various member countries? Our goal here is not to answer a question that is beyond our competence. It is quite clear that, with regard to our field of expertise (and with a European perspective), the United States is far from being an example in terms of social and environmental sustainability, not to mention identity and race issues. It is essential to abandon this reference to the United States as an inspiration for European construction and to instead imagine a new balance between mobility and rooting.

We consider that a critique of free movement applied to different types of mobility is not always reactionary and anti-liberal. Here, at the end of this book, we even consider it necessary in light of current events.

Overcoming the contradiction between the ultra-liberal doctrine of mobility and isolationist approaches means rethinking how we use the principle of the free movement of persons to strengthen social cohesion. It is not so much a question of calling this principle into question as of rethinking how we implement it.

When considering mobility from a transport and daily mobility standpoint, it seems reasonable to assume that regulatory measures are essential for ensuring fluidity: traffic and road safety rules are not designed to limit mobility but to optimize circulation. The same is true for the principle of the free movement of persons as applied to Europe. In a city, this principle does not mean that one can arrive everywhere at any time by any mode of transport. The difference between Europe and the United States is also significant in this respect: driving is perceived almost as a right in the United States, whereas in Europe this is less and less true (and in some cases not at all). In Europe, in fact, urban transport policies attempt to regulate the use of different modes of transport by focusing both on incentives and measures aimed at discouraging certain trips that fundamentally generate pollution with no real associated benefits. It goes without saying that internal tensions regarding mobility in Europe cannot merely be reduced to a problem of traffic engineering. Yet, this analogy is a reminder that a non-isolationist critique of mobility can limit the undesirable effects of mobility, both in cities and in Europe. Considering mobility in its different modalities, focusing on the question of the balance of benefits and drawbacks, and taking into account the tension between individual experience and mediated experience are the key ingredients of mobility policy. An obsession with free movement carries the risk of sacrificing integration as an essential component of European cohesion.

Is there an alternative model to the flat world American model? One that would be better suited to the European reality? This question prompted us to analyse the case of Switzerland (which was the subject of Chapter 7). Geographically situated at the heart of the European continent, Switzerland is characterized by a highly globalized economy and cosmopolitan society. Through a combination of *liberal*, *regulatory* and *localist* perspectives, we have looked at how Switzerland has succeeded in building a socio-territorial model that leaves significant room for territorial rooting, proximity and in some cases, even deceleration dynamics while enjoying the advantages of strong interconnectedness and a high level of internal and external exchanges thanks to mobility flows. Constitutionally speaking, Switzerland also stands out for its rights of referendum and popular initiative, which respectively allow citizens to challenge decisions taken by parliament and request a popular vote on an ad-hoc proposal through the collection of signatures. These rights exist at the national, regional (cantonal) and municipal levels and have been used regularly with regard to mobility issues (the free movement of people, goods or capital). This political system and the fact that actors must campaign for the items submitted to vote make Switzerland fertile ground for observing and identifying political rhetoric and controversies.

Can we consider Switzerland as an alternative and imitable model for rethinking a Europe beyond the question of mobility? The historical and geographical (size) differences are clearly great. However, we feel that, because of its federal tradition and experience managing diversity, the Swiss model has been widely regarded as a source of inspiration for European construction (Sidjanski, 1996). Some leading political scientists (Sidjanski, 2001, p. 12) have drawn an analogy between the two realities:

> For these good reasons, but wrongly, Switzerland has sometimes been proposed as a model for the European Union. In my opinion, Switzerland presents, as much by its qualities as by its defects, its lacunae and its efforts to adapt, a pilot experience and a miniature laboratory for the European Union.

More recently, the question was asked in a more direct way in a study entitled "Switzerland: A future model for the European Union? Similarities and differences" (Cheneval & Ferrín, 2017). The authors of this study also emphasize the fundamental difference between the European framework, which encourages the internal migration of people, and the Swiss case, where mobility was made possible but was implicitly discouraged in favor of preserving distinct territorial identities. Its solution for preserving its residential roots was to encourage long-distance commuting (Viry & Kaufmann, 2015). As Cheneval and Ferrín (Cheneval & Ferrín, 2017, p. 5) point out:

> It is of great interest that the one element in which the European Union has based the construction of EU citizenship and identity – mobility of residence – has been implicitly discouraged in Switzerland. . . . Most citizens identify with Switzerland as a country and they like it as it is, but they do not want to take advantage of their formal right to move to other parts of the country, especially not across language borders. . . . The Swiss compromise between the formal right and economic necessity of mobility on the one hand and the protection of political and cultural sub-identities on the other hand is commuting.

The authors leave the door open to a "Europe of commuters" which, by following the Swiss model, would help rebalance mobility and rooting.

This enthusiasm for long-distance commuting must be tempered, however, as long-distance commuting is difficult for those forced to accept it, as described in Chapter 4. Reflecting the obligation of mobility, long-distance commuting is generally accompanied by a fast-paced lifestyle and reinforces gender inequalities

(Drevon, Gerber, & Kaufmann, 2020; Drevon & Gumy, 2020; Viry & Kaufmann, 2015). In addition, our investigations in Switzerland have shown that high-intensity commuting generally results in a rejection of mobility due to issues of air pollution and traffic congestion. Furthermore, this work shows that a lack of rooting is associated with the spread of reversible mobility flows. Cross-border regions with a high rate of cross-border workers, for instance, must contend with the saturation of transport routes and often face economic imbalances and social tensions. Tourist flows, which are by definition reversible mobility, also threaten territorial roots and existing social relations in these destinations.

All of these observations suggest that a "Europe of commuters" modeled on a Switzerland of commuters is an option that offers some advantages as well as major disadvantages. In short, if mobility cannot be the watchword everywhere all of the time, it is not worth considering that reversibility can become the principle of application of free movement.

So, What Then?

The idea we have supported throughout this book is that mobility has been perceived and defended as a structuring principle of our societies everywhere and at all times, and thus as an absolute vector of the European integration process. Our idea was not to propose a radical critique of mobility or to deny its many benefits, but rather to challenge reductionist and simplifying perspectives that conceal the manifold issues associated with it. The management of the COVID-19 pandemic seems to have partially called these perspectives into question: mobility everywhere all the time is no longer the norm. Europe has also had to review rules that, until now, seemed immutable. In fact, in the face of the COVID-19 pandemic, we have seen enormous restrictions on mobility between EU countries.

In considering Switzerland, our goal was not to illustrate a case wherein mobility does not play a major role. What does interest us in the Swiss case, with all its qualities and defects, is the combination of approaches and ideologies that help define pragmatic positions regarding the management of different mobility flows in an incremental way, without taking a strong ideological stance (be it ultra-liberal or isolationist) beforehand. We feel that the country's successful management of diversity and development both economically and environmentally speaking are partially due to its ability to find a creative balance between the desire for mobility and the need for rooting. It is through a constant rebalancing of the benefits and issues associated with mobility flows that this rebalancing could be achieved elsewhere.

Mobility is ambivalent, as we have pointed out on many occasions and by showing it from multifaceted angles throughout this book. This ambivalence has a major consequence: the principle of free movement, a cardinal value of European construction, needs to be operationalized through a balanced conception of mobility in order to serve the cohesion of European construction and its reinforcement, not its disintegration. The real challenge for mobility policy is to become an instrument of redistribution for Europe's socio-spatial cohesion, and not of globalized capitalism. The diversity of Europe and the multiplication of spatial divisions within it (e.g., a country's more or less central or peripheral position in the urban system, the geography of languages, religious diversity, different lifestyles between the various European countries, etc.) requires an on the ground, detailed approach to mobility issues. Some cities and peripheral regions need to be more anchored to Europe and require increased reversible mobility. Other, more central ones, on the contrary, need to slow down the rhythm of life and focus more on local mobility. Some countries and regions are in need of stronger local (and thus rooted) development policy to avoid exodus and decline, while others require more migration (i.e., irreversible mobility). Generally speaking, targeted measures designed to fortify vulnerable populations are a must in terms of mobility and rooting, even in Europe's richest countries and regions.

Implementing such a policy by definition requires co-construction by local actors and the European institutional level, based for instance on a principle of subsidiarity. It also calls for a training policy that considers mobility as capital in keeping with a potential for action approach. If long-distance travel has become easier for those with means by grace of major transportation infrastructure and facilities, let us not forget that this ease of movement, in return, requires strong mobility skills, and therefore supposes being socialized or equipped. Moreover, our modern-day travel bulimia generates major environmental issues, namely atmospheric pollution due to greenhouse gas emissions. It is therefore not only a question of supporting those with mobility skills and equipping those without so that they may partake in this movement, but also of changing our relationship to travel and how we support individuals in changing their representations and actions. The expected transformation is therefore radical, fundamental and does not revolve around adapting modes of travel and/or uses to allow everyone to continue travelling just as much but with less pollution. What is certain today is that our newly acclaimed mobilities alone will not resolve the basic problems.

In the last chapter of his book *Down to Earth Politics in the New Climatic Regime*, Bruno Latour personally defended a revival of the European project. He stated (2018, pp. 102–103):

> If the first united Europe was created from below, on a base of coal, iron, and steel, the second will also come from below, from the humble matter of a somewhat durable soil. If the first united Europe was created to give a common home to millions of "displaced persons," as was said at the end of the last war, then the second will also be made by and for the displaced persons of today.

Seeking a new place for displaced persons seems a laudable political horizon for the revival of Europe. Different categories of people with different and contradictory reasons, from both inside and outside of Europe, seem to feel "displaced": people who moved or not but have experienced mobility in a negative way, people who suffered mobility and react against it. Seeking a safe haven for displaced people does not necessarily mean eradicating mobility but rather reconciling them with it by making the mobility experience more positive. We close this book by proposing the concept of resonant mobility, which can inspire institutional and other social actors in this quest for reconciliation.

In reaction to his own critique of modern dynamics of social acceleration (Rosa, 2013) and by avoiding a solution involving deceleration, Rosa proposed and extensively developed the concept of resonance. For him (2019, p. 174), "resonance is a kind of relationship to the world, formed through affect and emotion, intrinsic interest, and perceived self-efficacy, in which subject and world are mutually affected and transformed." A resonant experience is bidirectional (2019, p. 455): "it is not only about being touched, moved, gripped. . ., but also just as much about being self-efficacious and experiencing oneself as self-efficacious, i.e. reaching, touching, moving, and affecting something or someone oneself. . . . Only when both elements come together does a genuine resonant relationship emerge." In this respect, a resonant experience is directly related to the act of "encountering" and opposed to the idea of "conquering": "resonance means not merging in unity, but encountering another as an Other" (Rosa, 2019, p. 447).

Although mobility has, in the last decades, been clearly associated with social acceleration and the globalization disintegrating process, we argue that mobility is not by definition only that. On the contrary, mobility is also an essential dimension through which a resonant experience and the act of encountering the world and otherness can be forged. Resonant mobility as such can be characterized by three qualities: First, mobility must not be considered as an end in itself but rather as a sequence within an interrelated chain of situations aimed at creating an encounter. Second, mobility is not synonymous with social acceleration or increasing life rhythms, but instead is something that can be regulated to favor the quality of encounters. Behind the mirage of mobility as generator of rhythm (quicker, farther, more frequently, etc.), we have neglected mobility's capacity to create a meaningful environment. Third, resonant mobility must be considered not as unidirectional movement led by an active subject in an abstract space, but as a bidirectional dynamic in which the subject in movement and the socio-territorial environment need to co-participate in creating an encounter. In short, with the concept of resonant mobility, we would like to shift the focus from the principle of free movement to the ability to establish the encounter facilitated by mobility.

Is the idea of resonant mobility for a new European encounter radically new? Probably not. In the beginnings of the first united Europe, the challenges facing such encounters were very present. There was no simplistic solution, just real incremental politics. At some point, with the consolidation of the globalization process and the market as a reinvigorated utopia, the principle of free movement was increasingly presented as the ultimate solution for any difficulty in encountering others. The political message became simplistic and the understanding of mobility too restrictive. More recently, the effect of all of this has been a radical reaction against mobility. With the concept of resonant mobility, we would like to retrieve the original realism of the European project by highlighting the difficulties of establishing contact among people who themselves feel displaced. This is our humble contribution. It is no time for utopias; real mobility policies are needed for those who feel they have been set adrift.

References

Cheneval, F., & Ferrín, M. (2017). *Switzerland: A future model for the European Union? Similarities and differences*. https://doi.org/10.5167/UZH-136069

Drevon, G., Gerber, P., & Kaufmann, V. (2020). Dealing with daily rhythms: Families' strategies to tackle chronic time pressure. *Sustainability, 12*, 7193.

Drevon, G., & Gumy, A. (2020). Understanding multimodality through rhythm of life. In O. B. Jensen, C. Lassen, V. Kaufmann, M. Freudendal-Pedersen, & I. S. Gøtzsche Lange (Eds.), *Handbook of Urban Mobilities* (1st ed., pp. 367–377). London: Routledge.

Favell, A. (2008). *Eurostars and Eurocities: Free movement and mobility in an integrating Europe*. Malden, MA: Blackwell.

Kaufmann, V. (2014). *Retour sur la ville mobilité et transformations urbaines*. Lausanne: Presses polytechniques et universitaires romandes.

Latour, B. (2018). *Down to earth: Politics in the new climatic regime*. Cambridge, UK: Polity Press.

Recchi, E. (2015). *Mobile Europe: The theory and practice of free movement in the EU*. Basingstoke: Palgrave Macmillan.

Rosa, H. (2013). *Social acceleration: A new theory of modernity*. New York: Columbia University Press.

Rosa, H. (2019). *Resonance: A sociology of the relationship to the world*. Medford, MA: Polity Press.

Sidjanski, D. (2001). The Federal approach to the European Union (or the quest for an unprecedented European Federalism). *Notre Europe Research and Policy Paper, 14*. https://doi.org/10.2139/ssrn.283652

Sidjanski, D. (Ed.). (1996). *L'Union européenne à la lumière du fédéralisme suisse: Colloque Latsis 1995* (1st éd). Genève: Georg.

Viry, G., & Kaufmann, V. (Eds.). (2015). *High mobility in Europe: Work and personal life*. Houndmills, Basingstoke Hampshire: Palgrave Macmillan.

INDEX

Page numbers in *italics* indicate a figure and page numbers in **bold** indicate a table on the corresponding page.

For Product Safety Concerns and Information please contact our EU representative GPSR@taylorandfrancis.com
Taylor & Francis Verlag GmbH, Kaufingerstraße 24, 80331 München, Germany

www.ingramcontent.com/pod-product-compliance
Ingram Content Group UK Ltd.
Pitfield, Milton Keynes, MK11 3LW, UK
UKHW020000200926
475702UK00015B/2392
* 9 7 8 0 3 6 7 3 4 3 2 2 4 *